Virtual Subjects, Fugitive Selves

Fernando Pessoa and his Philosophy

JONARDON GANERI

OXFORD
UNIVERSITY PRESS

OXFORD
UNIVERSITY PRESS

Great Clarendon Street, Oxford, OX2 6DP,
United Kingdom

Oxford University Press is a department of the University of Oxford.
It furthers the University's objective of excellence in research, scholarship,
and education by publishing worldwide. Oxford is a registered trade mark of
Oxford University Press in the UK and in certain other countries

First Edition published in 2021

Impression: 1

Published in the United States of America by Oxford University Press
198 Madison Avenue, New York, NY 10016, United States of America

British Library Cataloguing in Publication Data
Data available

Library of Congress Control Number: 2020934980

ISBN 978–0–19–886468–4

Printed and bound by
CPI Group (UK) Ltd, Croydon, CR0 4YY

Contents

III. PESSOA PROVOKED

Preamble

Fernando Pessoa (1888–1935) has become many things to many people in the years that have passed since his untimely death. For some he is simply the greatest poet of the twentieth century, certainly in Portuguese and arguably more widely. His poetry, much loved and widely read, has over the years been meticulously edited, published, and translated. For others he has gradually emerged as a forgotten voice in twentieth-century modernism, now finally taking his rightful place alongside giants such as C. P. Cavafy, Franz Kafka, T. S. Eliot, James Joyce, and Jorge Luis Borges. And yet Pessoa was also a philosopher, and it is only very recently that the philosophical importance of his work has begun to attract the attention it deserves. Pessoa composed systematic philosophical essays in his pre-heteronymic period, defending rationalism in epistemology and sensationism in the philosophy of mind. His heteronymic work, decisively breaking with the conventional strictures of systematic philosophical writing, is a profound and exquisite exploration in the philosophy of self.

What I shall attempt to do here is to pull together the strands of this philosophy and to rearticulate it in a way that does justice to its breathtaking originality. I have found that I need to repurpose tools and techniques in contemporary philosophy of mind, and also that in many places Pessoa's philosophy of self goes far beyond anything in current theory. Pessoa made two great discoveries about consciousness: the existence of heteronymic subjectivity, and the possibility of multiplicity in the subject position. His leading concern is with their implications for the metaphysical grounding of individual subjects of experience. His investigation of the problem is brilliant, original, and multifaceted. It is multifaceted in the particular sense that each of the literary genres he writes in is associated with a distinct approach to its solution. There are his heteronymic and intersectionist experiments in poetry, his prose antinovel *The Book of Disquiet*, his formal philosophical essays, and his neopaganist notes. In each of these genres the problem of the grounding of subjects is explored from a different angle, and, indeed, different solutions are proposed.

I will demonstrate the extraordinary explanatory power of Pessoa's theory by applying it to the analysis of some of the trickiest and most puzzling problems about the self to have appeared in the global history of philosophy. It will turn out that in doing so we shall need to extend Pessoa's philosophy in ways even he did not imagine.

Acknowledgments

Heartfelt thanks to my two research assistants, Austin Simoes-Gomes and Rodrigo Luque, and to the audiences at talks where some of the ideas presented here have been rehearsed, including the Philosophy Departments at Yale University and the University of Virginia, the Institute for Comparative Literature and Society, Columbia University, the Humanities program at Yale University, and Ashoka University's lecture series at the India International Centre, New Delhi. Particular thanks to David Jackson, Bartholomew Ryan, Nicolas Bommarito, and to two anonymous readers for Oxford University Press, all of whose comments have been very helpful indeed. Thanks too to New York University for a Global Research Initiative Fellowship (September to December 2018), the release from teaching duties affording me the opportunity to prepare a full first draft, and to the support and encouragement of my colleagues in the Philosophy Department.

Selections from Richard Zenith's translations of Pessoa's poems are reprinted courtesy of the translator by permission of SLL/Sterling Lord Literistic Inc. and Penguin Random House LLC, © Richard Zenith. Yasumasa Morimura's *An Inner Dialogue with Frida Kahlo (Hand Shaped Earring)*, 2001, © Yasumasa Morimura, is reprinted courtesy of the artist and Luhring Augustine, New York.

Jonardon Ganeri

New York

List of Illustrations

PART I
PESSOA PRESENTED

1

Pessoa's Novel Invention

Fernando Pessoa's invention of the heteronym represents a singular moment in the history of subjectivity.[1] Scattered among his drafts of prefaces to never-to-be-completed editions of his writings and in letters to friends and editors are the few explicit clues we possess as to his intentions. 'The mental origin of my heteronyms lies in my restless, organic tendency to depersonalization and simulation,' he writes, exactly isolating the twin poles around which his philosophy of self revolves, before continuing, 'Fortunately for me and others, these phenomena have been mentally internalized, such that they don't show up in my outer, everyday life among people; they erupt inside me, where only I experience them.'[2] Each heteronym is fully and in its own right a person:

> Ever since I was a child, I've felt the need to enlarge the world with fictitious personalities—dreams of mine that were carefully crafted, envisaged with photographic clarity, and fathomed to the depths of their souls...I intensely conceived those characters with no need of dolls. Distinctly visible in my ongoing dreams, they were utterly human realities for me, which any doll—because unreal—would have spoiled. They were people.[3]

Pessoa's three most famous heteronyms are the world-class poets he names Alberto Caeiro, Álvaro de Campos, and Ricardo Reis: 'I placed all my power of dramatic depersonalization in Caeiro; I placed all my mental discipline, clothed in its own special music, in Ricardo Reis; and in Álvaro de Campos

---

[1] Excellent recent overviews of Pessoa in English include: Jackson, David. *Adverse Genres in Fernando Pessoa*. Oxford, 2010, pp. 3–27; Maunsell, Jerome Boyd. 'The hauntings of Fernando Pessoa'. *Modernism/Modernity* 19 (2012), pp. 115–37; and Frow, John. *Character and Person*. Oxford, 2014, pp. 214–25.

[2] Letter to Adolfo Casais Monteiro, 13 January 1935. In *The Selected Prose of Fernando Pessoa*, edited and translated by Richard Zenith. Grove Press, 2007, p. 254.

[3] [Another version of the genesis of the heteronyms], *Selected Prose*, pp. 261–2. Square brackets indicate a title supplied by the editor.

Virtual Subjects, Fugitive Selves: Fernando Pessoa and his Philosophy. Jonardon Ganeri, Oxford University Press (2021). © Jonardon Ganeri.
DOI: 10.1093/oso/9780198864684.001.0001

I placed all the emotion that I deny myself and don't put into life.'[4] As he puts it in a draft preface for an unfinished edition of the *Fictions of the Interlude* (his designation for the complete corpus of his poetic work),

> In the case of the authors of *Fictions of the Interlude*, it is not only the ideas and feelings which differ from mine: the technique of composition itself, the very style, differs from mine. In those instances each protagonist is created as essentially different, not just differently thought out. For this reason, poetry is predominant in *Fictions of the Interlude*. In prose, it is more difficult to other oneself.[5]

Heteronymy is, as the name implies, an othering of oneself, an awareness of oneself but as other. The contrast with the pseudonym is deliberate: 'Pseudonymous works are by the author in his own person, except in the name he signs; heteronymic works are by the author outside his own person. They proceed from a full-fledged individual created by him.'[6] A pseudonym is a mask, a disguise intended, even if only ironically, to hide the true identity of the author. A heteronym is something else entirely: it is the author writing 'outside his own person' and in doing so transforming himself into an other I. A heteronym occupies the first-person position within the experience of the author, and has a defined literary voice and a distinctive power of expression. So to 'write in the name of'[7] a heteronym is not to hide oneself behind a mask but to live in experience as that very person; each heteronym, Pessoa says, is 'lived by the author within himself' and has 'passed through his soul'.[8] A heteronym is 'someone in me who has taken my place'.[9]

In assuming a heteronym one transforms oneself into an other I: 'First we must create another I, charged with suffering—in and for us—everything we suffer.'[10] The experiences of my heteronym are both *in* me, in the sense

---

[4] Letter to Adolfo Casais Monteiro, 13 January 1935, *Selected Prose*, pp. 253–4.

[5] [Preface to *Fictions of the Interlude*], *Selected Prose*, p. 313.

[6] [Bibliographical summary], in *A Little Larger than the Entire Universe: Selected Poems*, edited and translated by Richard Zenith. Penguin, 2006, p. 3.

[7] [Bibliographical summary], *A Little Larger*, p. 5.

[8] [Aspects], in *Selected Prose*, p. 2.

[9] *The Book of Disquiet*, edited and translated by Richard Zenith. Penguin, 2002, sketch #351. All references to *The Book of Disquiet* will follow the numbering in Zenith's Portuguese and English editions. The online *LdoD Archive* provides, among other things, for cross-referencing against different editions of the *Livro do Desassossego*. In what follows any citation attributed to Pessoa from *The Book of Disquiet* should be understood as an attribution to his semi-heteronym Bernardo Soares, the book's protagonist.

[10] 'Sentimental education', *The Book of Disquiet*, p. 455.

that I am their host, and also *for* me, standing, with respect to me, in a first-personal subjective relationship. When Pessoa writes of heteronymy that it is a subjective state in which 'every felt pain is automatically analysed to the core, ruthlessly foisted on an extraneous I..',[11] he exactly formulates the essence of the concept in the idea of experience that is at once irreducibly first-personal and yet also alien. A heteronym is a fully formed subject subsisting within one's conscious experience. Heteronyms are, to introduce a notion I will have much more to say about later, *virtual subjects*, subjects which are 'well-defined personalities who have incorporeally passed through [one's] soul.'[12] Unlike the target of empathy, which would occupy a second-person position, addressed as 'you', the formal feature that is definitive of heteronymy is that a heteronym occupies the first-person position, spoken of with a use of the first-person pronoun 'I'. Nor is heteronymy reducible to the first-person plural, for 'we' is a pronoun semantically inclusive of both you and I. A heteronym possesses agency, if only in the capacity to compose verse, and has its own expressive and experiential style. A heteronym is another I, an I who is not me, an othered I:

> But since I am me, I merely take a little pleasure in the little that it is to imagine myself as that someone else. Yes, soon he-I, under a tree or bower, will eat twice what I can eat, drink twice what I dare drink, and laugh twice what I can conceive of laughing. Soon he, now I. Yes, for a moment I was someone else: in someone else I saw and lived this human and humble joy of existing as an animal in shirtsleeves.[13]

Heteronymic simulation is, we might say, the mechanism of self-alienation.

If transforming oneself in simulation into another I is the core of the idea of heteronymic subjectivity, an equally important theme in Pessoa is that of depersonalization. Living through a heteronym, which from one point of view must certainly constitute an enrichment of experiential life, is paradoxically described in terms of a loss of self: 'Today I have no personality: I've divided all my humaneness among the various authors whom I've served as literary

---

[11] 'Sentimental education', *The Book of Disquiet*, p. 456.
[12] [Aspects], in *Selected Prose*, p. 2. I will say more about the notion of a virtual subject in the chapters 'Heteronyms as virtual subjects' and 'Virtual subjects'. I am not alone in appealing to the language of the virtual to elucidate heteronymy: David Jackson calls the heteronyms 'virtual authors' (*Adverse Genres*, p. 15) and John Frow describes them as 'virtual selves' (*Character and Person*, p. 222).
[13] *The Book of Disquiet*, #374.

executor. Today I'm the meeting-place of a small humanity that belongs only to me...I subsist as a kind of medium of myself, but I'm less real than the others, less substantial, less personal, and easily influenced by them all.'[14] Again, 'I created a non-existent coterie, placing it all in a framework of reality. I ascertained the influences at work and the friendships between them, I listened in myself to their discussions and divergent points of view, and in all of this it seems that I, who created them all, was the one who least there.'[15]

Several distinct claims are intertwined here. The first is that even as he assumes multiple heteronyms Pessoa is separately conscious of himself in the capacity of medium or meeting place for them. Unlike a heteronym, which corresponds to a well-defined style of experiencing, this separate self-consciousness is one that is empty of any specific personality or content: it is a depersonalized self-awareness. The use of the first person in relation to this type of self-consciousness is thus quite distinct from that which figures in the self-expression of a heteronym (the use made of it in the formula 'an extraneous I'). Second, one's awareness of oneself as medium or meeting place is less robust than one's awareness of oneself as another I, in the sense that it does not sustain as strong a sense of presence. Finally, one's self-awareness as medium or meeting place is associated with a clearly identifiable trait: it at least partially consists in a capacity to observe the heteronyms, both from the outside ('I *see* before me, in the transparent but real space of dreams, the faces and gestures of Caeiro, Ricardo Reis and Álvaro de Campos'),[16] and also, more importantly, from the inside, a partly introspective and partly empathetic capacity to analyse and scrutinize the subjective character of the heteronymic mental life being lived through.

It seems, then, that two distinct kinds of self-awareness are co-present in any act of heteronymic simulation: a *heteronymic* self-awareness which consists in an awareness of oneself as another I, living through a distinctive set of experiences, emotions, and moods; and what I will call a *forumnal* self-awareness, an awareness of oneself as hosting the heteronym, which is at the same time a place from which one's experiential life qua heteronym can be observed and analysed. It is from the first-person position of the forum that Bernardo Soares, the semi-heteronymic/semi-orthonymic narrator of *The Book of Disquiet*, speaks: 'For me it's never I who thinks, speaks or acts. It's always one of my dreams, which I momentarily embody, that thinks, speaks

---

[14] [Another version of the genesis of the heteronyms], *Selected Prose*, p. 262.
[15] Letter to Adolfo Casais Monteiro, 13 January 1935, *Selected Prose*, p. 257.
[16] Letter to Adolfo Casais Monteiro, 13 January 1935, *Selected Prose*, p. 257.

and acts for me. I open my mouth, but it's I-another who speaks. The only thing I feel to be really mine is a huge incapacity, a vast emptiness, an incompetence for everything that is life.'[17] Pessoa describes Bernardo Soares as a *semi*-heteronym because 'his personality, although not my own, doesn't differ from my own but is a mere mutilation of it. He's me without my rationalism and emotions. His prose is the same as mine, except for certain formal restraint that reason imposes on my own writing.'[18] And 'Bernardo Soares' is also a semi-*orthonym* because the name is a 'mere mutilation' of 'Fernando Pessoa', 'Bernardo' differing from 'Fernando' in only two letters, and 'Soares' is almost exactly a syllabic inversion of 'Pessoa'.[19] When Pessoa-as-Soares writes that 'due to my habit of dividing myself, following two distinct mental operations at the same time, it's generally the case that as I lucidly and intensely adapt myself to what others are feeling, I simultaneously undertake a rigorously objective analysis of their unknown self, what they think and are,'[20] he shows a keen understanding of the co-presence of these two kinds of self-awareness, a simulated heteronymic self-awareness consisting in 'adaption' to the feelings of another I, and a forumnal self-awareness consisting in 'objective analysis' of what is thereby felt.

The formal structure of Pessoa's philosophy of self is nowhere more clearly set out than in his celebrated late poem *Countless Lives Inhabit Us*:

> Countless lives inhabit us.
> I don't know, when I think or feel,
> Who it is that thinks and feels.
> I am merely the place
> Where things are thought and felt.
> I have more than just one soul.
> There are more I's than I myself.
> I exist, nevertheless,
> Indifferent to them all.
> I silence them: I speak.
> The crossing urges of what

---

[17] *The Book of Disquiet*, #215.
[18] Letter to Adolfo Casais Monteiro, 13 January 1935, *Selected Prose*, p. 257.
[19] A different semi-orthonym exists as an entry in *The Transformation Book*: 'Ferdinand Sumwan (= Fernando Pessoa, since Sumwan = Some one = Person = Pessoa) A normal, useless, lazy, careless, weak individual.' Pessoa, Fernando. *The Transformation Book*, edited and translated by Nuno Ribeiro. Contra Mundum Press, 2014, p. 326.
[20] *The Book of Disquiet*, #305.

> I feel or do not feel
> Struggle in who I am, but I
> Ignore them. They dictate nothing
> To the I I know: I write.[21]

When I think or feel, the first stanza says, it is one of many possible I's that is thinking or feeling. This heteronymic use of 'I' is immediately juxtaposed with another use of 'I', to refer to the place where things are thought or felt. The second stanza continues with this use, for it is only from the position of the forum that I can affirm that I have more than one soul—each heteronym, taken individually, thinks of itself as a single unified self. The two uses of 'I', heteronymic and forumnal, are again juxtaposed in the final stanza, the urges felt or unfelt are the felt volitions of a heteronym—that is, of myself qua another I—but I (qua forumnal observer) disregard them.

The poem's disconcerting air of paradox is a deliberate construct, produced by the alternation without explicit indication of two quite distinct uses of 'I'. There is a third use too, almost too pedestrian for Pessoa to mention, the standard and everyday use of 'I' to refer indexically to whomsoever it is that has spoken or written it: as when Pessoa writes in a letter to a friend, 'I submitted the copies required by the Office of Propaganda.'[22] In the poem there is perhaps a trace of this third, indexical use in the echoing phrases 'I speak' and 'I write'.

The disconnect between the heteronymic and the forumnal can be heard playing out in another poem, in which 'who I am', my heteronymic self, is contrasted with 'what I am', myself as forum:

> I don't know who my soul is.
> Nor does it know who I am.
> Understand it? It would take time.
> Explain it? Don't know if I can.
> And in this misunderstanding
> Between who I am and what am I
> There's a whole other meaning
> Lying between earth and sky.[23]

---

[21] *Fernando Pessoa & Co.: Selected Poems*, edited and translated by Richard Zenith. Grove Press, 1999, p. 137. The poem is dated 13 November 1935, just two weeks before Pessoa's death on the 30th.

[22] Letter to Adolfo Casais Monteiro, 13 January 1935, *Selected Prose*, p. 252.

[23] *A Little Larger*, p. 329.

2
Heteronyms as Virtual Subjects

The authorial act of heteronymic self-transformation is quite different from that of inventing a character in a story. Pessoa alludes to the difference when, while noting that novelists and playwrights 'often endow the characters of their plays and novels with feelings and ideas that they insist are not their own', he adds somewhat gnomically that in the authorship of heteronyms 'the substance is the same, though the form is different.'[1] What is fundamental to the notion of a heteronym is that it is an othered I, 'lived by the author within himself', that is to say, lived first-personally. So a heteronym is not a character because the relationship an author stands in to an invented character is a third-personal one. The point in question is analogous to the one William James makes when he says that 'it is impossible to reconcile the peculiarities of our experience with our being only the absolute's mental objects...Objects of thought are not things *per se*. They are there only for their thinker, and only as he thinks them. How, then, can they become severally alive on their own accounts and think themselves quite otherwise than as he thinks them? It is as if the characters in a novel were to get up from the pages, and walk away and transact business of their own outside of the author's story.'[2] The autonomy here denied to fictional characters is a freedom from the author who has created them. James's point is that if an individual human subject were merely the 'mental object' of another mind, standing in the same relationship to this mind as the fictional character does to its author, it would similarly be without a capacity for autonomous self-expression. The comparison helps to clarify what is so distinctive and original in the idea of heteronymy. For a heteronym is not a mental *object* but a mental *subject*, a virtual subject transforming its author into

---

[1] [Aspects], *Selected Prose*, p. 1.

[2] James, William. *A Pluralistic Universe: Hibbert Lectures*. Floating Press, 1909, p. 69. There is an exquisite treatment of this very issue in chapter 31 of Unamuno's 1914 novel *Mist*. Here, a character begs the author to be permitted to live, but to no avail: the author has already decided that he must die. Unamuno, Miguel de. *Mist*, translated by Warner Fite. University of Illinois Press, 1955.

Virtual Subjects, Fugitive Selves: Fernando Pessoa and his Philosophy. Jonardon Ganeri, Oxford University Press (2021). © Jonardon Ganeri.
DOI: 10.1093/oso/9780198864684.001.0001

another I: 'Why should I look at twilights if I have within me thousands of diverse twilights...and if, besides seeing them inside me, I myself *am them*, on the inside and the outside?'[3]

Stephen Crites, by contrast, says of Søren Kierkegaard's pseudonyms that nobody 'would mistake them for the voices of real human beings. They are altogether theatrical creations. They are sheer personae, masks without actors underneath, voices.'[4] Kierkegaard does, sometimes, describe his pseudonyms—which he also calls 'polyonyms'—in a manner that makes them sound more similar to heteronyms than conventional pseudonyms. He is keen to stress that he is simply their producer, or the occasion for their production, or a prompter (*souffleur*) for them, but not their author: 'What is written is indeed therefore mine, but only so far as I have put the life-view of the creating, poetically actualized individuality into his mouth in audible lines, for my relation is even more remote than that of a poet, who creates characters and yet in the preface is himself the author. For I am impersonally, or personally, in the second person, a souffleur who has poetically produced the authors.'[5] Yet he goes on to deny that he is himself any of his pseudonyms, and says that he has 'no opinion about them except as third party'; remarks which imply that a Kierkegaardian pseudonym is also still a third party and not an essentially first-personal 'another I'. Pessoa's heteronyms, as John Frow, puts it, 'are not personae, masks through which the poet speaks; they are autonomous figures which allow him to take on quite distinct personalities in his writing.'[6] Polyonyms, again, are multiple names for the same thing, and they give rise to puzzles of their own, most famously the puzzle of explaining how identity statements containing them can be informative. Solutions to that puzzle, such as distinguishing between the reference of a name and its sense, the mode under which the reference is presented,[7] are of little help, however, in understanding the phenomenon of heteronymy, for a heteronym is another I, not the same I under another mode of presentation.

One of Pessoa's most basic philosophical concerns is with what I shall refer to as 'the grounding problem for subjects'. This is the problem of

---

[3] *The Book of Disquiet*, #215.

[4] Crites, Stephen. 'Pseudonymous authorship as art and act'. In *Kierkegaard: A Collection of Critical Essays*, edited by Josiah Thompson. Anchor Books, 1972, pp. 183–229, at p. 216.

[5] Kierkegaard, Søren. 'A first and last declaration'. In *Concluding Unscientific Postscript*, translated by Alastair Hannay. Cambridge, 2009, pp. 527–31, at pp. 527–8.

[6] Frow, John. *Character and Person*. Oxford, 2014, p. 215.

[7] Frege, Gottlob. 'On sense and reference'. In Geach, Peter, and Black, Max, eds., *Translations from the Philosophical Writings of Gottlob Frege*. Oxford: Blackwell, 1960, pp. 56–78.

accounting for the metaphysical grounds for individual subjects of experience: what it is they exist in virtue of; what they are due to; what they are
dependent on for their being.[8] The invention of heteronymy serves to under-
line the fact that there is no solution to this problem in attempts to reduce
subjects to merely intentional objects, such as are the characters in a novel.

A closer, if still inadequate, analogy would be with one of those stories in
which each section has a different narrator writing from a first-person position, such as Orhan Pamuk's novel *My Name is Red*, or William Faulkner's
As I Lay Dying, or Ryūnosuke Akutagawa's short story *In a Grove*, on which
Akira Kurosawa's film *Rashōmon* is based.[9] Each character in one of these
stories presents in the first person and is not merely reported on from a
third-personal perspective. Each one takes it in turn to occupy the narrator
position. Yet a sequence of distinct narrators writing in the first person is
still not a display of heteronymy. They are distinct characters taking it in
turn to speak about themselves in the first person; there is no suggestion
that any of them is identical to the author, and neither can any be described
as the author transformed into another I.

Nor does Jorge Luis Borges yet explicitly describe heteronymy in his brilliant story *The Circular Ruins*.[10] In this story someone, whom Borges
describes only as 'the foreigner', sets out to dream into existence another
human being, having understood 'that the task of moulding the incoherent
and dizzying stuff that dreams are made of is the most difficult work a man
can undertake.' Within his directed dreamworld he fashions a youth, whom
Borges describes as a 'phantasm' and a 'simulacrum', an individual who is
'not a man but the projection of another man's dream'. Pessoa too describes
the creation of heteronyms as acts of directed imagining, but the distinction
between a simulation and a simulacrum is crucial. For there is no suggestion at any point in Borges's story that the dreamt-up simulacrum is the
foreigner himself—another I of the dreamer—which is what would be

---

[8] As a term of art in contemporary philosophy, grounding refers to a particular sort of non-
causal and asymmetric priority between facts, indicated by the use of expressions like 'in virtue
of', 'due to', 'based on', 'what makes', and 'because of'. See Correia, Fabrice, and Schnieder,
Benjamin, eds. *Metaphysical Grounding: Understanding the Structure of Reality*.
Cambridge, 2012.

[9] Pamuk, Orhan. *My Name is Red*, translated by Erdağ M. Göknar. Faber & Faber, 2001.
Faulkner, William. *As I Lay Dying*. Random House, 1990. Ryūnosuke Akutagawa, *Rashōmon
and Other Stories*, translated by Kojima Takashi. Tuttle Publishing, 2011.

[10] Borges, Jorge Luis. *Collected Fictions*, translated by Andrew Hurley. Penguin, 1999,
pp. 96–100.

required if the simulacrum, a virtual object, were to be a heteronym, a virtual subject, a simulated occupant of the subject position.

Borges ends the story with a twist: the foreigner is given to understand that he is himself a simulacrum, as 'with relief, with humiliation, with terror, he realized that he, too, was but appearance, that another man was dreaming him'. It is within the dream of another man that the foreigner exists, exists as a simulacrum, and in the phrase 'he, too, was but appearance' there is again a clear implication that what is being created is a merely intentional object. The simulacra in these directed dreams, as the characters in a novel, are virtual objects; whereas a virtual *subject* is a simulation, a heteronym, a transformation of the author into another I.

Pessoa anticipates Borges when he writes, 'I begin to wonder if I exist, if I might not be someone else's dream. I can imagine, with an almost carnal vividness, that I might be the character of a novel, moving within the reality constructed by a complex narrative, in the long waves of its style.'[11] What is important to appreciate, though, is that Pessoa is not offering this as a description of heteronymic subjectivity; it is the simpler idea that one might discover that one is, after all, a simulacrum oneself. The grounding problem for subjects begins with the assumption that subjects are not merely apparent, and yet, reluctant to grant them the status of fundamental pieces of the world's furniture, asks what their existence is dependent on. We are more like shadows than hallucinations.

There is in fact in *The Circular Ruins* a trace of the idea of heteronymy, but it is not to be found in the relationship between 'the foreigner' and his dreamt-up simulacrum. When Borges writes, 'the foreigner dreamed that *he* was in the centre of a circular amphitheatre', the embedded use of the personal pronoun situates the foreigner within his own dream. When one dreams it is not uncommon for one to oneself figure in the dream, as the one to whom the events in the dream are presenting. The 'subject-within-the-dream' is both a virtual subject and a simulation of the dreaming subject; and for this reason it would be entirely appropriate to describe the subject-within-the-dream as the dreaming subject's heteronym in the dream. Evan Thompson, in his magnificent book *Waking, Dreaming, Being*,[12] uses the language of virtual-reality

---

[11] *The Book of Disquiet*, #285. Borges, it would seem, wrote *The Circular Ruins* and other stories in the same series in the late 1930s. He spent six weeks in the summer of 1924 living in Lisbon, and this has led to some speculation that Pessoa and he may have met. Ferrari, Patricio. 'Pessoa and Borges: In the margins of Milton'. *Variaciones Borges* 40 (2015), pp. 3–21.

[12] Thompson, Evan. *Waking, Dreaming, Being: Self and Consciousness in Neuroscience, Meditation and Philosophy*. Columbia, 2014.

gaming to make the interesting suggestion that the distinction between subject-within-the-dream and dreaming subject is analogous to the distinction between an avatar in a virtual world and its user: 'We need to distinguish between the dreaming self and the dream ego—between the self-as-dreamer and the self-within-the-dream,' he rightly says, continuing,

> In a nonlucid dream, we identify with our dream ego and think,' I'm flying'. In a lucid dream, we think, 'I'm dreaming', and we recognize that the dreaming self isn't the same as the dream ego, or how we appear within the dream. The dream ego is like an avatar in a virtual world; the dreaming self is its user...In a nonlucid dream, we lose the awareness that we're imagining things and identify with the dream ego as the I. We're like gamers who identify so completely with their avatars they forget they're gaming. In a lucid dream, we regain awareness of our imagining consciousness. Nonlucid dreams frame experience from the imagined perspective of the dream ego; lucid dreams reframe experience from the perspective of the imagining and dreaming self. Lucidity can enable the dreaming self to act consciously and deliberately in the dream state through the persona of the dream ego, who becomes like an avatar in a role-playing game....[13]

It is not, though, quite correct to characterize the relationship between the dreaming subject and the subject-within-the-dream as being that there are two distinct subjects whose distinctness is overlooked in an act of mistaken identification. The foreigner dreams that *he* is in a circular amphitheatre and there is no question of an error due to misidentification.[14] It is not that in his dream a certain simulacrum is in the amphitheatre, a simulacrum which is mistaken by the dreamer to be himself. So the analogy breaks down, and instructively so, for the way it does so helps us to understand better the difference between avatars and heteronyms. The difference is that an avatar is a virtual object, a simulacrum, but the subject-within-the-dream is a virtual subject, a virtual occupant of the subject position. What it means to be at the subject position within the dream is indeed that the dream experience is 'framed from the perspective' of this position, and by positioning himself there the dreamer has in effect created a heteronym, an 'I' within the dream. So he cannot 'use' this

---

[13] Thompson, *Waking, Dreaming, Being*, pp. 109–10.
[14] On the philosophical concept of error due to misidentification, and immunity thereof, see Prosser, Simon, and Recanati, François, eds., *Immunity to Error through Misidentification: New Essays*. Cambridge, 2012.

heteronym as a gamer might an avatar or a master might a slave, because he does not stand in an appropriately third-personal relationship to it. It is literally correct to say 'In *my* dream *I* was flying', and this statement is not a mistaken rendering, based on a false identification with another, of 'In my dream my avatar was flying'.

The idea of heteronymy is much better captured in Yasumasa Morimura's multiple self-portraiture under the assumed identities of famous historical artists, if indeed Morimura would be willing to affirm 'I myself am them, on the inside and the outside'. As in *My Name is Red*, the text for his video piece *Egó Sympósion* has every participant, each of whom is a famous figure in the history of art, taking turns to speak for themselves in the first person. The reason this does not reduce to a case of sequential first-person narration by a series of distinct narrators, and the reason it is not merely a case of successive pseudonymous disguise, is that the viewer is never in any doubt that it is Morimura who is assuming—that is, simulating—each participant in turn. Though made up to resemble Frida Kahlo (see Figure 2.1) or Johannes Vermeer, Morimura makes no attempt to hide himself or to pretend not to be there. The representation is of Morimura-as-Kahlo not Morimura-as-if-Kahlo, not Morimura pretending to be Kahlo.

The Portuguese novelist José Saramago provides a superb illustration of the idea of the heteronym in a short notebook entry about Pessoa. He

Figure 2.1   Yasumasa Morimura, *An Inner Dialogue with Frida Kahlo (Hand Shaped Earring)*, 2001, © Yasumasa Morimura, courtesy of the artist and Luhring Augustine, New York.

imagines Pessoa looking in a mirror and seeing his reflection, in turn as Reis, as Caeiro, and as Campos. 'My name is Ricardo Reis', 'My name is Alberto Caeiro', 'My name is Álvaro Campos', he declares in turn. When he looks again later that night, the mirror image he sees is that of his own face. 'My name is Bernardo Soares', he says, invoking an almost-orthonym:

[O]n one of those days when Fernando passed in front of a mirror he spied in it, at a glance, another person. He thought this was just another optical illusion, those ones that happen when you're not paying attention, or that the last glass of *eau de vie* had not agreed with his liver and his head, but he cautiously took a step back just to make sure that—as is usually assumed—when mirrors show something they do not make mistakes. This one, however, had indeed made a mistake: there was a man looking out at him from inside the mirror, and that man was not Fernando Pessoa. He was a little shorter, and his face was somewhat dark-skinned and completely clean-shaven. Unconsciously Fernando brought his hand to his upper lip, then breathed deeply in childlike relief: this moustache was still there. One can expect many things from an image that appears in a mirror, but not that it will speak. And because these two, Fernando and the image that wasn't an image of him, were not going to stay watching one another forever, Fernando Pessoa said, 'My name is Ricardo Reis.' The other man smiled, nodded, and disappeared. For a moment the mirror was empty, bare, then right away another image appeared, of a thin, pale man who looked as if he were not long for this world. It seemed to Fernando that this must have been the first one; however, he made no comment, merely saying, 'My name is Alberto Caeiro.' The other did not smile; he merely nodded slightly, agreeing, and left. Fernando Pessoa waited, having always been told that whenever there are two a third will always follow. The third figure took a few seconds to arrive, and he was one of those men who look as if they have more health than they know what to do with, and he had the unmistakable air of an engineer trained in England. Fernando said, 'My name is Álvaro de Campos,' but this time he did not wait for the image to disappear from the mirror, but moved away from it himself, probably tired from having seen so many people in such a short space of time. That night, in the small hours of the morning, Fernando Pessoa awoke wondering whether Álvaro de Campos had stayed in the mirror. He got up, and what he found there was his own face. So he said, 'My name is Bernardo Soares,' and went back to bed.[15]

---

[15] Saramago, José. *The Notebook*, translated by Amanda Hopkinson and Daniel Hahn. London, Verso, 2010, pp. 24–5.

Morimura writes, analogously, 'Let me begin by introducing the participants: Leonardo da Vinci, Michelangelo Merisi da Caravaggio, Diego Velázquez, Rembrandt Harmensz. van Rijn, Jan van Eyck, Albrecht Dürer, Élisabeth Louise Vigée Le Brun, Johannes Vermeer, Vincent van Gogh, Frida Kahlo, Marcel Duchamp, Andy Warhol, and finally me, Yasumasa Morimura.'[16] When each of the artists then speaks in the first person, it is Morimura-as-Kahlo, as-Duchamp, as-van Gogh who speaks. In finally introducing 'Yasumasa Morimura', it is his orthonym he is introducing rather than merely himself, just as the last mirror image in Saragamo's analogy is the semi-orthonymous Bernardo Soares and no longer a mere reflection of Pessoa. In situating himself, a Japanese male, in the subject position of a range of European painters, and even, in other works, in the subject position the European gaze assigns to the Asian female, Morimura exploits heteronymy to investigate topics of identity and perception in a fascinating and original manner.[17]

A heteronym, finally, let me be completely clear, is not a Cartesian soul. A Cartesian soul is a putative denizen in the actual world, an immaterial mental substance standing in some mysterious relationship with other real entities such as human bodies. Lacking in spatial location, there is nothing to pair particular souls with particular effects: if two souls simultaneously acquire or lose a certain property, there is no way, even in principle, to decide which of the two is the cause of some subsequent event. This is what Jaegwon Kim calls the 'pairing problem' for Cartesian souls.[18] Then there is, as Bernard Williams puts it, 'absolutely nothing left to distinguish any Cartesian "I" from any other, and it is impossible to see any more what would be subtracted from the universe by the removal of *me*.'[19] A heteronym is an aspect of a virtual world, although, as we have seen, it is not a virtual object like an avatar. What is subtracted from the universe by the removal of a heteronym is an entire style of feeling, and styles of feeling are also what is added to the universe by the invention of new heteronyms.

[16] Morimura Yasumasa, Original screenplay for *My Art, My Story, My Art History—A Sympósion on Self-Portraits. Egó Sympósion.* Japan Society, New York, 2018, pp. 148–59.
[17] I thank Maria Slautina for alerting me to the importance of the heteronymic mechanism to the art-historical interpretation of Morimura's self-portraiture.
[18] Kim, Jaegwon. 'Lonely souls: causality and substance dualism'. In Corocan, Kevin, ed., *Soul, Body, and Survival: Essays in the Metaphysics of Human Persons.* Cornell, 2001, pp. 30–43.
[19] Williams, Bernard. 'Imagination and the self'. In his *Problems of the Self.* Cambridge, 1973, pp. 26–45, at p. 42.

3

The Enigma of Heteronymy

Speaking of the 'adverse genres of virtual authorship' that the system of heteronymy sustains, David Jackson describes the interpreter's task as being 'to discern how Pessoa's writings in different genres and under the guise of *other selves*, the heteronyms he invented, allowed him, the mythical creator of himself, both to be *and* not to be. Pessoa's "startling paradox"…is that he could only be Pessoa when he was not Pessoa.'[1] This is exactly so, allowing that extreme caution must be exercised in using the phrase 'other selves' to describe the heteronyms, for this phrase can easily be misunderstood as making a second- or third-personal reference to selves other than myself. Heteronymy, the simulation of another I, on the other hand, is, as I have stressed, fundamentally a phenomenon of the *first-person* singular. Jackson is right to emphasize that there is something paradoxical, or at least oxymoronic, in the phrase 'another I'. What can another I be other than an I that is other than myself, an I that is not I? Let me call this the 'enigma of heteronymy.'

Pessoa himself presents the enigma in a very succinct way. 'Never do I feel so Portuguese,' he says, 'as when I feel that I am different from me— Alberto Caeiro, Ricardo Reis, Álvaro de Campos, Fernando Pessoa, and as many more as have been or will be.'[2] The puzzle is that feeling that I am different from me seems to be as little a possibility as feeling that red is not red, or that a pain is not a pain. How can what is apparently a logical *impossibility* be an *experiential* possibility? Several formulations in *The Book of Disquiet* exactly manifest the form of the enigma. Pessoa, as Soares, says, 'I live off impressions that aren't mine. I'm a squanderer of renunciations, someone else in the way I'm I.'[3]. Embedded in this is the formula 'I'm someone else in the way I'm I', which logically entails 'I'm not myself in the way I'm I' or 'I'm not I in the way I'm I'. In two more formulations the concept of

---

[1] Jackson, David. *Adverse Genres in Fernando Pessoa*. Oxford, 2010, p. 15, my italics.
[2] Quadros, António, and da Costa, Dalila Pereira, eds., *Obra Poética e em Prosa*. Lello & Irmão Editores, 1986, vol. 2, p.1014.
[3] *The Book of Disquiet*, #93.

Virtual Subjects, Fugitive Selves: Fernando Pessoa and his Philosophy. Jonardon Ganeri, Oxford University Press (2021). © Jonardon Ganeri.
DOI: 10.1093/oso/9780198864684.001.0001

a heteronym is reduced to its most basic essence: 'Once again I'm I, exactly as I'm not';[4] and, 'We are who we're not.'[5] Surely, though, and this is the puzzle, 'an I that is not I' is a direct affront to the law of identity. 'If I'm even different from my own identical self, how can I be identical to a completely different self?'[6] wonders Soares, non-rhetorically.

If Pessoa's concept of simulation is the source of one enigma, his notion of depersonalization gives rise to another, equally vexing, puzzle. A passage from *The Book of Disquiet* recapitulates the idea that there are two uses of the first person and the inherent tension in their application:

> I've created various personalities within. I constantly create personalities. Each of my dreams, as soon as I start dreaming it, is immediately incarnated in another person, who is then the one dreaming it, and not I. To create, I've destroyed myself. I've so externalized myself on the inside that I don't exist there except externally. I'm the empty stage where various actors act out various plays.[7]

A heteronym is an externalization of oneself on the inside, not another, distinct self but one's own self made other—that's the paradoxical use of the first person in 'I'm not I'. Its second use is exemplified in the statement 'I'm the empty stage', the forum where the I's that are not I meet and a position from which they are scrutinized. Pessoa puts the matter very sharply when he describes forumnal self-awareness as a harbour: 'I harbour in me, like unwanted souls, the very philosophies I criticize. Omar could reject them all, for they were all external to him, but I can't reject them, because they're me.'[8] Pessoa affirms, paradoxically, that in creating the heteronyms he has destroyed himself: 'From so much self-revising, I've destroyed myself.'[9] Insofar as what this appears to say is both that Pessoa exists and that he doesn't, that he is both personified and depersonalized, it is a flagrant violation of the law of non-contradiction.

So the two poles around which Pessoa's entire philosophy of self revolves are commitments to two extremely enigmatic propositions:

Simulation: I am a subject other than the subject I am.

Depersonalization: I am merely a forum for the subject I am.

---

[4] *The Book of Disquiet*, #436.   [5] *The Book of Disquiet*, #95.
[6] 'The river of possession', *The Book of Disquiet*, p. 450.   [7] *The Book of Disquiet*, #299.
[8] *The Book of Disquiet*, #448.   [9] 'Self-examination', *The Book of Disquiet*, p. 451.

The first of these seems to violate the law of identity, if it has the same logical form as 'Pessoa is someone other than Pessoa'. The second seems to state that Pessoa is both a depersonalized venue and a personal subject, and so to have the form 'Pessoa is both φ and not φ', a violation of the law of non-contradiction. What I am calling the enigma of heteronymy is the challenge to provide an analysis of the functions of the first person, that is to say, the use or uses of the pronoun 'I' and so of the phenomenology of self-consciousness, according to which this pair of propositions is not trivially false but, on the contrary, interestingly and importantly true.

Let me say, by way of terminological stipulation, that Pessoa *assumes* a heteronym in simulation and that he *sustains* a heteronym in depersonalization. The word 'inhabit' is broad enough in its semantic reach to include both these notions, but, as I will show later, it would be a mistake to attempt to reduce one to the other. There are two distinct types of use of 'I' and two distinct types of self-consciousness. Assuming one heteronym, Pessoa is a pantheistic naturalist poet Caeiro; assuming another heteronym, he is a neo-classical poet Reis; assuming a third, he is the hedonistic Campos. When he assumes the semi-heteronym 'Bernardo Soares', he is a solitary philosopher of self-consciousness, and he is an alienated rationalist when he assumes the orthonym 'Fernando Pessoa'. Each such heteronym is not Pessoa and yet is Pessoa. As the sustainer of heteronyms, Pessoa's self-awareness is as of being a place, a stage, a forum for these various subjects of experience, and when Pessoa identifies himself with the forum, he has the impression that he has depersonalized himself. The phenomenology of forumnal self-awareness is one of emptiness. Insofar as he is nevertheless aware of himself in the capacity of being one of the available subjects, that is to say, that there is a compresent dimension of heteronymic self-awareness, he finds himself in the paradoxical situation of both being and not being a subject.

Pessoa seems to have used his unconstituted antinovel *The Book of Disquiet* as a literary vehicle wherein he could wrestle with this puzzle: 'This book is a single state of soul, analysed from all sides, investigated in all directions.'[10] 'I doubt that any outwardly human creature has lived their consciousness of self in a more complex fashion... This book is not by him; it is him.'[11] For the book's protagonist the central existential challenge is this:

All of a sudden, as if a surgical hand of destiny had operated on a long-standing blindness with immediate and sensational results, I lift my gaze

[10] *The Book of Disquiet*, #194.   [11] *The Book of Disquiet*, p. 466.

from my anonymous life to the clear recognition of how I live...All that I've done, thought or been is a series of submissions, either to a false self that I assumed belonged to me because I expressed myself through it to the outside, or to a weight of circumstances that I supposed was the air I breathed. In this moment of seeing, I suddenly find myself isolated, an exile where I'd always thought I was a citizen. *At the heart of my thoughts I wasn't I.* I'm dazed by a sarcastic terror of life, a despondency that exceeds the limits of my conscious being. I realize that I was all error and deviation, that I never lived, that I existed only in so far as I filled time with consciousness and thought.[12]

I should pause here to set aside a solution to the enigma which some interpreters of Pessoa have found tempting. The enticing solution is to deny that Pessoa is rational. Perhaps it is not the case that the possibilities he claims to be able to access in imagination are indeed experiential possibilities; rather, he is merely under an illusion that they are. To put it another way: has Pessoa made a fundamental discovery about the nature of subjectivity, or is he in the grip of a psychosis? It is clear though, first of all, that the depersonalization Pessoa is talking about does not satisfy the diagnostic criteria of the eponymous mental disorder. As a clinical illness, depersonalization disorder is characterized as a lack of affective response, as relating to one's body as if it were an automaton, and as a cause of distress and functional impairment. A Pessoan self would only partially qualify as satisfying Criterion A in the diagnostic list provided in the American Psychiatric Association's *Diagnostic and Statistical Manual of Mental Disorders*: 'Experiences of unreality, detachment, or being an outside observer with respect to one's thoughts, feelings, sensations, body, or actions (e.g., perceptual alterations, distorted sense of time, unreal or absent self, emotional and/or physical numbing).'[13] Pessoa claims, to the contrary, that his affective life is greatly enriched by his experiments with heteronymy. Criterion B states that '[d]uring the depersonalization or derealization experiences, reality testing remains intact', and Criterion C that the 'symptoms cause clinically significant distress or impairment in social, occupational, or other important areas of functioning.' Pessoan depersonalization is indeed associated with factors such as being an outside observer of one's mental processes

---

[12] *The Book of Disquiet*, #39, my italics.
[13] DSM-5: *The Diagnostic and Statistical Manual of Mental Disorders*. American Psychiatric Association, 2013, §300.6.

and of no longer feeling oneself, but the key indicators of depersonalization disorder, such as loss of affective meaning, derealization, and bodily automaticity, are all notably absent from Pessoa's extensive self-descriptions.

It is instructive to contrast Pessoa's self-description of his subjective state with the one provided by Yayoi Kusama, another exceptionally creative, intelligent, imaginative, and introverted artist. Kusama has been clinically diagnosed with the mental illness of depersonalization disorder. In her autobiography she provides a vivid first-personal description of her condition, saying,

> I feel as if I am in a place where pleated, striped curtains completely enclose me, and finally my soul separates from my body. Once that happens, I can take hold of a flower in the garden, for example, without being able to feel it. Walking, it is as if I am on a cloud; I have no sense of my body as something real. In the midst of that fuzzy state when the soul seems to have separated, all sense of time is lost ... [T]he horrible suffering of depersonalisation is much greater than the pain of any reality: a hellish reality is still better than the experience of losing yourself, the world, and time. It is terrible seeing existence annihilated. At least in reality you get a solid sense of the self that is suffering.[14]

Kusama's first-personal account emphasizes many of the features commonly associated with depersonalization disorder, including emotional numbing, bodily automaticity, derealization, distorted sense of time, and functional impairment. Clinicians emphasize, in addition, that the symptoms of depersonalization disorder include that 'the patient feels that he is no longer himself, but he does not feel that he has become someone else. The condition is, therefore, not one of so called transformation of personality.'[15] The key phenomenological descriptors are that

> the patient may say his feelings are 'frozen', that his thoughts are strange; his thoughts and acts seem to be carried on mechanically as if he were a machine or automaton. People and objects appear unreal, far away, and lacking in normal colour and vividness. The patient may say he feels as if he were going about in a trance or dream. He appears perplexed and bewildered because of the strangeness of unreality feelings. He has

---

[14] Kusama, Yayoi. *Infinity Net: The Autobiography of Yayoi Kusama*. Tate Publishing, 2011.
[15] Noyes, A. P., and Kolb, L. *Modern Clinical Psychiatry*. Philadelphia, 1964 (6th edn.), p. 84.

difficulty in concentrating and may complain that his brain is 'dead' or has 'stopped working'.[16]

Little in this phenomenological description is true of Pessoa. Pessoan depersonalization is the outcome of the application of a philosophical method, a method, as I shall later call it, of analytical phenomenology. What Pessoa means by 'depersonalization' is a discovery in the logic of self-consciousness and not the aberration of a dysfunctional mind.[17] In this he is following in the footsteps of Henri-Frédéric Amiel, who coined the term 'depersonalization' in his journal:

> I find myself regarding existence as though from beyond the tomb, from another world; all is strange to me; I am, as it were, outside my own body and individuality; I am depersonalized, detached, cut adrift. Is this madness? No. Madness means the impossibility of recovering one's normal balance after the mind has thus played truant among alien forms of being, and following Dante to invisible worlds. Madness means incapacity for self-judgment and self-control. Whereas it seems to me that my mental transformations are but philosophical experiences. I am tied to none. I am but making psychological investigations.[18]

Contemporary philosophers of psychiatry agree that a characteristic of a genuine mental disorder is that it is something over which the sufferer has little or no control.[19] Pessoa refers to Amiel several times,[20] and his experiences too are 'philosophical experiences', under the direction of his guided imagination.

---

[16] Noyes and Kolb, *Clinical Psychiatry*, p. 84.

[17] On one point Kusama and Pessoa do agree about symptoms: both claim to experience synaesthesia, that is, for example, to be able to smell and taste colours or see smells. *Selected Prose*, p. 67.

[18] Amiel, Henri-Frédéric. *Fragments d'un journal intime*, vol. 2. Paris, 1884; entry for 8 July 1880. Translated as *Amiel's Journal* by Mary A. Ward. New York, 1889, p. 353.

[19] Graham, George. *The Disordered Mind*. London: Routledge, 2010, p. 45.

[20] See, for example, *The Book of Disquiet*, ##72, 119, 340, 475. Pessoa's annotated copy of the first volume of Amiel's journal is preserved in the Casa Fernando Pessoa. The second volume, with the entry from which I quote, is, however, unfortunately not among the extant volumes of his personal library.

4

The Multiplicity of I

If in heteronymic simulation I am a subject other than the subject I am, there are evidently as many other I's as there are possible acts of simulation. Pessoa, inhabiting countless lives, says that by creating in imagination a multiplicity of virtual subjects, each of which is him, he has 'ubiquitized' himself: 'I live in their dreams, their instinctive nature, and their body and its postures all at the same time. In a sweeping, unified dispersion, I ubiquitize myself in them, and at each moment of our consciousness I create, and am, a multitude of selves—conscious and unconscious, analysed and analytical—joined together as in a spread fan.'[1] So he affirms a thesis I will call 'Subject Plurality':

Subject Plurality: I am many subjects other than the subject I am.

'By delving within, I made myself into many,' he says.[2] We need, though, to distinguish two versions of this thesis, for it can be read as making either a diachronic claim or a synchronic one. The diachronic claim is that Pessoa *successively* assumes a plurality of different heteronyms, first Caeiro, then Reis, then Pessoa himself, or any other sequence from the many heteronyms he has created:

Successive Subject Plurality: I am sequentially many subjects other than the subject I am.

As one of his most famous poems, written under his own name, begins:

> I don't know how many souls I have
> I've changed at every moment.[3]

---

[1] *The Book of Disquiet*, #305.   [2] *The Book of Disquiet*, #93.
[3] *Selected Poems*, p. 243.

Virtual Subjects, Fugitive Selves: Fernando Pessoa and his Philosophy. Jonardon Ganeri, Oxford University Press (2021). © Jonardon Ganeri.
DOI: 10.1093/oso/9780198864684.001.0001

My identity over time, Pessoa in effect says, is protean: a succession of different virtual subjects, each of which is me, occupies the subject position.
'And so I do not evolve, I simply journey... I continuously change personality....'[4] Why is this a description of a single, albeit protean, person rather
than a succession of distinct persons? What blocks its collapse into another
version of serial first-personal narration, like Pamuk's *My Name is Red*? We
shall need to discover, and have yet to do so, what is it that enables Pessoa to
say that each one is him, which means finding a solution to the enigma of
heteronymy; but we can at least note for now that if it is true that each heteronym is sustained in forumnal self-awareness, then it might, in addition,
be the case that every heteronym is sustained by one and the same forum.
So when Pessoa writes, later in the same poem,

> That's why I read, as a stranger,
> My being as if it were pages [,]

the sequence of heteronyms ('my being') is likened to the successive pages
of a book, and the first person in 'I read' is here used to refer to forumnal
self-awareness, now compared with a reader, a single persisting observer of
the sequence of heteronymic subjects. The principle in question is this one:

Forum Singularity: I am a single forum for the many subjects I am.

Forum Singularity is what justifies the use of metaphors like 'meeting-place'
and 'harbour' in relation to the forum: while every ship has its own berth,
the harbour is their common place. Another metaphor, of longer proven-
ance, is to liken the relationship between forumnal and heteronymic self-
awareness to the ocean and the multiple waves it sustains: 'And so, in this
universal river / Where I'm not a wave, but waves, I languidly flow, with no
requests / And no gods to hear them.'[5]
   One of Pessoa's most startling claims, though, is that he can assume multiple heteronyms *simultaneously*. Pessoa describes this as the most difficult
accomplishment of the imagination:

> To visualise the inconceivable in dreams is one of the great triumphs that
> I, as advanced a dreamer as I am, only rarely attain. To dream, for example,

---

[4] Letter to Adolfo Casais Monteiro, 20 January 1935. *Selected Prose*, p. 263.
[5] *A Little Larger*, p. 117.

that I'm simultaneously, separately, severally the man and the woman on a stroll that a man and a woman are taking along the river. To see myself—at the same time, in the same way, with equal precision and without overlap, being equally but separately integrated into both things—as a conscious ship in a South Sea and a printed page from an old book. How absurd this seems! But everything is absurd, and dreaming least of all.[6]

Again, 'The highest stage of dreaming is when, having created a picture with various figures whose lives we live all at the same time, *we are jointly and interactively all of those souls*. This leads to an incredible degree of depersonalization and the reduction of our spirit to ashes....'[7] What these passages affirm is a synchronic reading of Subject Plurality:

Simultaneous Subject Plurality: I am simultaneously many subjects other than the subject I am.

Pessoa is certainly aware that subjects cannot simply be synthesized, that it is not the case that one is simultaneously many subjects because one is a single subject which is their amalgamation: 'Between one and another soul lies the impassable chasm of the fact that they're two souls.'[8] It would thus be quite wrong to argue that the simultaneity in question is achieved through a combination of distinct virtual subjects into a single virtual subject that subsumes them. For just as two distinct perspectives cannot be combined to produce a single, third perspective that is their mereological sum, so two distinct subject positions cannot be combined to produce a single, third subject position that is their synthesis.[9] The claim must rather be that I am such that in these circumstances I am simultaneously many subjects at once.

There is a considerable temptation to employ a collective noun to describe the state of affairs Simultaneous Subject Plurality provides for. Pessoa does so once himself, albeit with a rather specific intention:

---

[6] *The Book of Disquiet*, #157.

[7] 'The art of dreaming for metaphysical minds', *The Book of Disquiet*, p. 405.

[8] *The Book of Disquiet*, #363. Pessoa's 'impassable chasm' echoes William James' talk of an 'absolute breach' between personal minds.

[9] The impossibility of mereologically combining subjects, qua bounded phenomenal unities, has been noted by contemporary philosophers writing about panpsychism. See, for example, Coleman, Sam. 'The real combination problem: panpsychism, micro-subjects, and emergence'. *Erkenntnis* 79 (2014), pp. 19–44.

Each of us is several, is many, is a profusion of selves. So that the self who disdains his surroundings is not the same as the self who suffers or takes joy in them. In the vast colony of our being there are many species of people who think and feel in different ways. At this very moment, jotting down these impressions during a break that's excusable because today there's not much work, I'm the one who is attentively writing them, I'm the one who is glad not to have to be working right now, I'm the one seeing the sky outside, invisible from in here, I'm the one thinking about all this, I'm the one feeling my body satisfied and my hands still a bit cold. And my entire world of all these souls who don't know each other casts, like a motley but compact multitude, a single shadow—the calm, bookkeeping body with which I lean over Borges's tall desk, where I've come to get the blotter that he borrowed from me.[10]

The intention, here, is to refer to the fact that conscious experience is unified although comprised of many sorts of phenomenal input: attention, mood, perception, cognition, and proprioception. Commentators on and interpreters of Pessoa have been drawn by such remarks to present the Pessoan self as a sort of parliament of souls. Consider, for example, Antonio Tabucchi, who in his novel *Pereira Declares* has Dr Cardosa explaining to Pereira a 'confederation of souls' theory:

[T]o believe in a 'self' as a distinct entity, quite distinct from the infinite variety of all the other 'selves' that we have within us, is a fallacy, the naïve illusion of the single unique soul we inherit from Christian tradition, whereas Dr. Ribot and Dr. Janet see the personality as a confederation of numerous souls, because within us we each have numerous souls, don't you think, a confederation which agrees to put itself under the government of one ruling ego.[11]

Despite Pessoa's appeal, once, to the metaphor of a colony—and there only in connection with the phenomenal unity of consciousness rather than with reference to the multiplicity of heteronyms—the 'confederation' theory is not Pessoa's. It is a Proustian, not a Pessoan, picture of multiplicity, Marcel Proust reflecting on 'those innumerable and humble "selves" that compose

---

[10]   *The Book of Disquiet*, #396.
[11]   Tabucchi, Antonio. *Pereira Declares*, translated by Patrick Creagh. New Direction, 1997, p.76.

our personality' and referring to 'a truly objective truth...namely that none of us is single, that each of us contains many persons who do not all have the same moral value'.[12] The reason that the multiplicity of heteronyms is not properly thought of as a confederation of souls is that heteronymic multiplicity is essentially first-personal. We must not fall into the error of thinking that the phrase 'another I' introduces a self in a second- or third-personal manner, a distinct self other than I to whom I may stand in some second- or third-personal relationship, as one soul does with another in a confederation or a meeting of friends. Pessoan multiplicity is the more difficult and radical idea that the first-person position itself sustains multiplicity, that every heteronym is another I. The idea is exactly captured in the lines of *Countless Lives*: 'I don't know how many souls I have...Attentive to what I am and see, I *become* them and stop being I.' Again, in this remarkable passage, Pessoan multiplicity is clearly irreducible to a confederation:

And as I pass by those houses, villas, and chalets, I also live the daily lives of all their inhabitants, living them all at the same time. I'm the father, mother, sons, cousins, the maid and the maid's cousins, all together and all at once, thanks to my special talent for simultaneously feeling various and sundry sensations, for simultaneously living the lives of various people— both on the outside, seeing them, and on the inside, feeling them.[13]

What is affirmed here is the experiential possibility of simultaneously being many I's; it is not the idea of being an I that consists in a collection of other selves. While Proust's multiplicity reflects Nietzsche's thought that there are distinct and discrete personae, coexisting either in harmony or else in tension, within a single human psyche, Pessoa's multiplicity rests on the radical and possibly even absurd idea that '[i]t would be interesting to be two kings at the same time: not the one soul of them both, but two distinct, kingly souls.'[14]

An appreciation of this distinction is crucial to seeing why Pessoa's multiplicity of I is not reducible to another mental illness, multiple personality

---

[12] Proust, Marcel. *Remembrance of Things Past*, translated by C. K. Scott Moncrieff and Terence Kilmartin. Random House, 1982, p. 605.

[13] *The Book of Disquiet*, #299.

[14] *The Book of Disquiet*, #404. For Pessoa's divergence from Nietzsche in this matter, see Visser, Rehan. 'Fernando Pessoa's art of living: ironic multiplicities, multiple ironies'. *Philosophical Forum* 50 (2019), pp. 435–545.

disorder. Tabucchi, indeed, makes the confederation theory sound exactly like this disorder when he continues,

> What we think of as ourselves, our inward being, is only an effect, not a cause, and what's more it is subject to the control of a ruling ego which has imposed its will on the confederation of souls, so in the case of another alter ego arising, one stronger and more powerful, this ego overthrows the first ruling ego, takes its place and acquires the chieftainship of the cohort of souls.[15]

In sufferers of multiple personality disorder (MPD) there is a multiplicity of so-called 'alters', each with its own personality traits, practical agendas, and continuity conditions.[16] The alters take turns in having executive control over the body, each meanwhile having its own personality. Joanna Courteau has associated Pessoan multiplicity with her romanticization of mental illness, which she describes using another metaphor, that of a tribe. If multiple personality disorder is the condition that 'we each harbour the entire range of human possibilities. Within each of us there is a tribe with a complete cycle of legends and dances,' she suggests that 'Fernando Pessoa's heteronymous and orthonymous poetry can be viewed as the expression of just such an attempt to give voice to the tribesmen within. Pessoa anticipated in art by sixty years the multiple-personality theory of science. He shows through the heteronyms and the orthonyms that it is possible to be aware of each member of one's tribe...'[17]

Yet consider the testimony of Doris Fischer, where three alters—RD, SD, M—alternate in who has executive control over the body (that is, is 'out'):

> SD watched when RD was out. There would be three of us watching her, each with thoughts of her own. SD watched RD's mind, M watched SD's thoughts of RD, and I watched all three...When RD was out...SD saw her thoughts directly. M saw them through SD. By 'through' I mean as reflected from SD. There was scarcely any difference in the time of SD's and M's getting them. And besides, M saw SD's own thoughts directly.

---

[15]   Tabucchi, *Pereira Declares*, p. 77.

[16]   See Radden, Jennifer. 'Multiple selves'. In Gallagher, Shaun, ed., *The Oxford Handbook of the Self*. Oxford, 2011, pp. 548–71.

[17]   Courteau, Joanna. 'The quest for identity in Pessoa's orthonymous poetry'. In Moneiro, George, ed., *The Man who Never Was: Essays on Fernando Pessoa*. Gavea-Brown Pubns, 1982, pp. 93–108, at p. 96.

This was generally the case with M, but there were times when SD was so far in that M got RD's thoughts directly. This was seldom. I don't know why it was. As for me, I saw RD's thoughts as they were reflected by M, and besides I saw M's own thoughts directly. This was the case before SD went [i.e. disappeared], but after she went I saw, as I do now, RD's thoughts directly. SD was a barrier that prevented me from seeing them that way as long as she lasted, but now the barrier is removed.[18]

The alters of Doris Fischer are asymmetrically aware of each other's mental states, sometimes directly so and sometimes indirectly, when cognitive access is mediated by another alter. Just as, in *My Name is Red,* there is a series of selves each taking it in turn to be the narrator, so, in multiple personality disorder, there is a confederation of selves, each taking it in turn to be 'out', that is, in executive control of the body. All this is a far cry from Pessoa's simultaneous subject plurality: there is no counterpart, for a sufferer of MPD, of the directed lucidity in simulation or the detachment in analytical self-observation that constitute Pessoa's philosophical experience. What is absent from Doris Fischer's description, more particularly, is the suggestion, crucial to heteronymy, that any alter can conceive of a second alter as 'another I'. RD does not think, 'I will be M'; rather, RD is simply replaced by M. And although M can 'see' SD's thoughts, they are not seen *as her own* but as the thoughts of someone else, SD. There is a particular use of the first person, which I will later describe as the *fugitive* use of 'I', which is unavail-able to a sufferer of MPD or in a 'confederation' of selves.

Nor does Pessoan multiplicity satisfy the diagnostic criteria for multiple personality disorder. The dominant markers are discontinuity in the sense of self and sense of agency, and gaps in memory recall. The most recent ver-sion of the American Psychiatric Association's *Diagnostic and Statistical Manual of Mental Disorders* emphasizes that a diagnosis of mental disorder is appropriate only when the symptoms cause distress or dysfunction and have no more natural explanation:

A. Disruption of identity characterized by two or more distinct personal-ity states, which may be described in some cultures as an experience of possession. The disruption in identity involves marked discontinuity in sense of self and sense of agency, accompanied by related alterations in

---

[18] Testimony from a 1916 case study, cited in Braude, Stephen. *First Person Plural.* Routledge, 1991, pp. 69–70.

affect, behaviour, consciousness, memory, perception, cognition, and/or sensory-motor functioning. These signs and symptoms may be observed by others or reported by the individual. B. Recurrent gaps in the recall of everyday events, important personal information, and/or traumatic events that are inconsistent with ordinary forgetting. C. The symptoms cause clinically significant distress or impairment in social, occupational, or other important areas of functioning. D. The disturbance is not a normal part of a broadly accepted cultural or religious practice. In children, the symptoms are not better explained by imaginary playmates or other fantasy play.[19]

Part of the new emphasis is not to diagnose mental illness when the phenomenon is better seen as a normal part of 'a broadly accepted cultural or religious practice'. Pessoa sometimes does exploit the metaphor of describing himself, insofar as he can be called their author, as merely a 'medium' through which the heteronyms express themselves,[20] yet he is evidently not 'possessed' by a heteronym as if by a spirit, for he wilfully and through an act of directed imagination assumes one. His construction of a model of mind through an application of the philosophical method of directed, analytical simulation in fact provides a powerful tool for understanding what is at stake in such cultural and religious practices.

What we need is a model of the *ordered* mind that makes it intelligible how genuine mental *disorders* like MPD are possible, and what they consist in. Rather than trying to 'diagnose' Pessoa as the victim of a mental illness,[21] it is better to appreciate the ways in which his complex account of the *functional* self can help in reaching a better understanding of a spectrum of dysfunctionalities. Stephen Braude, in his book *First Person Plural*, comes closest to applying something like a Pessoan analysis of functioning subjectivity to the understanding of MPD as a dysfunction, Braude describing every alter as a discrete 'apperceptive centre', a centre of self-awareness to which thoughts are indexed.[22] The subject plurality of which Pessoa speaks is also that of a multiplicity of apperceptive centres and not that of a multiplicity in the occupation of a single apperceptive centre. What sufferers

[19]   DSM-5: *The Diagnostic and Statistical Manual of Mental Disorders*. American Psychiatric Association, 2013, §300.

[20]   *Selected Prose*, pp. 2, 262.

[21]   As does, to give still another example, Greg Mahr: Mahr, Greg. 'Pessoa, life narrative, and the dissociative process'. *Biography* 21 (1998), pp. 24–9.

[22]   Braude, Stephen. *First Person Plural*. Routledge, 1991, pp. 77–83.

from MPD lack is the guarantee, which exists in a functional self, that Subject Plurality provides for, that I am the many subjects I am. One might conjecture, for instance, that in such disorders there is a breakdown in Forum Singularity: no single forumnal self-awareness, no awareness of one-self as the harbour for the multiple heteronymic identities one can assume. Also absent in MPD is any sense that the subjective simulations are under the control of the simulating subject, that they are 'philosophical experiences.'

The distinction I am highlighting, between successive and simultaneous subject plurality, has found a surprising application: understanding Afrofuturism's experimentation with multiple sonic selves. According to the musicologist Kodwo Eshun, what is distinctive about Afrofuturism is the producer's embrace of a multiplicity of parallel sound identities, this in con-trast with the classic rock and pop musician's attraction to serial musical personae. Thus, while David Bowie assumed in turn the identities of Major Tom, Aladdin Sane, and the Thin White Duke, where in each case abandon-ing or destroying the earlier persona was intrinsic to musical innovation, an Afrofuturist producer like Underground Resistance, Kool Keith, 4hero, or Juan Atkins holds many sonic selves ('machine names') in play at once. Eshun appeals directly to the notion of a heteronym to make sense of this:

> The machine name is not a pseudonym, a fake name. Rather it's is a het-eronym, a many-name, one in a series of parallel names which distributes and disperses you into the public secrecy of open anonymity. I is a crowd: the producer exists simultaneously, every alterego an advertisement of myselves...Children, instinctive animists, identify with toys and dolls, subjecting themselves to and projecting onto the Inanimate: every 12-year-old knows that I is an other and another and another. In the 70s, the Bowie heteronyms—Major Tom, Aladdin Sane, Thin White Duke— were serial. Now heteronyms come in parallel. Today, the Futurist pro-ducer is always greater than one, always multiplying into omni-duos, simultaneously diverging selves that never converge into knowledge of self.[23]

[23] Eshun, Kodwo. *More Brilliant than the Sun: Adventures in Sonic Fiction.* Quartet Books, 1999, 07[106]–07[107]. I thank Sreerag Jyothish for drawing my attention to this discussion.

There remains an unfortunate valorization of mental disorder in Eshun's thinking about sequential heteronymy, and an echo of the Proustian model of self as confederation:

> Instead of putting the scientific self back together or mending the broken fragments of cybernetic psyche, Kool Keith heightens what used to be called schizophrenia, intensifies the crackup and the breakdown. The self doesn't slit up or multiply into heteronyms. Rather, the self no longer amputates itself down to a single part but instead asserts that I is a crowd, that the human is a population of processes.[24]

This is, nevertheless, an intriguing application of Pessoa's discovery. It aims to bring out a unique and distinctive value of simultaneous heteronymy, that the creation of a new self in subjective simulation does not have to predicated on the destruction of the old one. That is a point Trace Reddell has emphasized: 'For Eshun, Juan Atkins' multiple identities avoid the pitfalls of the pseudo-heteronymity of artists like David Bowie, Bob Dylan or Madonna, who made a career of rather dramatic shifts in persona and presence.'[25] There is a clear suggestion, in all these passages, that the Afrofuturist embrace of simultaneous machine names is an improvement on rock and pop experimentation with protean musical personhood. What it has to do with, perhaps, is a new understanding of the constitutive principles that are involved in musical creativity, that it is a mistake to suppose that a precondition for the emergence of one sonic self is the death of another.

---

[24] Eshun, *More Brilliant than the Sun*, 03[027]–03[028].
[25] Reddell, Trace. 'Ethnoforgery and outsider Afrofuturism'. *Dancecult: Journal of Electronic Dance Music Culture* 5 (2013), pp. 88–112, at pp. 97–8.

5

Intersecting Horizons

Pessoa, we have seen, says, 'the highest stage of dreaming is when, having created a picture with various figures whose lives we live all at the same time, *we are jointly and interactively all of those souls*',[1] and again that 'It would be interesting to be two kings at the same time: not the one soul of them both, but two distinct, kingly souls.'[2] How are we to imagine a situation in which I am simultaneously yet severally multiple subjects?

Many contemporary writers on personal identity have said that one can imagine a scenario involving the fission of a person, a situation where as a result of division what was up to that moment a single person subsequently continues as two distinct people. The topic of fission in personal identity is an area where thought experiments rule supreme. One can imagine, for instance, that the left and right hemispheres of a person's brain are transplanted into two separate bodies, each of which then has all the memories and opinions and character traits of the person whose brain has been bisected. Or one can imagine a teletransporter or 'resurrection machine' which creates an exact duplicate of the person who steps into it, memories and all, at another place, possibly vaporizing the body of the person who stepped into the machine in the process.[3] Perhaps, indeed, the teletransporter develops a fault and creates two exact duplicates, each of whom steps out in the other place. The individual who is about to be divided might well wonder 'Which one will I be?' and there seems to be no easy answer to that question.

One solution to the challenge of multiple embodiment is to defend the view that persons are individuals of a special sort, higher-order individuals somewhat akin to kinds. The kind *tiger* is a higher-order individual in the sense that it is constituted at various times by different populations of ordinary individual tigers. Higher-order individuals like the kind *tiger* are distinct from properties such as tigerness, and are also distinct from the populations that constitute them. The reason is that we can talk about kinds

---

[1] 'The art of dreaming for metaphysical minds', *The Book of Disquiet*, p. 405.
[2] *The Book of Disquiet*, #404.   [3] Lem, Stanisław. *Dialogi*. Kraków, 1957, Dialog I.

Virtual Subjects, Fugitive Selves: Fernando Pessoa and his Philosophy. Jonardon Ganeri,
Oxford University Press (2021). © Jonardon Ganeri.
DOI: 10.1093/oso/9780198864684.001.0001

in ways we cannot talk about their members or the corresponding proper-ties: 'The tiger is on the endangered species list'; 'The tiger is scattered throughout south and southeast Asia, its number recently increasing.' So a kind has a distinctive spatio-temporal spread, coming into existence and possibly going out of existence at specific times, distributed over specific regions, and so on. Might one not, similarly, say that a person is an individ-ual but of a higher-order sort, so that the person who before fission was singly embodied is now, after fission, spread across two bodies?

Another sort of higher-order individual is a word-type, and, just as with kinds, words are constituted by tokens, individual utterances or inscriptions of that word, and so have a certain spatial distribution and temporal spread. Words have their own life histories, and we have little difficulty in thinking of them as individuals, albeit individuals of an abstract sort, as for example when we make lists of them in dictionaries. With a nod to the multiplicity of heteronyms, Pessoa seemingly likens himself to a higher-order individual when he says, 'Having made myself into what I am—at worst a lunatic with grandiose dreams, at best not just a writer by an entire literature...'[4] He is using 'literature' here as a literary-kind term to denote the higher-order indi-vidual whose members are his heteronymic writers of poetry and prose. This literary entity (to which, indeed, one might give the company name 'Pessoa & Co.') came into existence at a particular moment, has a certain, evolving population, and its life story has followed a certain well-documented route.

And yet the deeper issue is not metaphysical but phenomenological, and it isn't a puzzle about the multiple embodiment of a single person but about a person's simultaneous embrace of multiple first-person positions. (To see the contrast, consider that successive subject plurality is actually the exact inverse of resurrection, which is the idea that even as I discard one body I take up another. Successive subject plurality is the different idea that even as this body discards one I it takes up another I.) One philosopher has put for-ward an argument which, if sound, would imply that Pessoa's 'highest stage of dreaming' does not, in fact, present a phenomenological possibility. 'Imagine my situation facing division. I look ahead. I anticipate. What do I anticipate? The answer, it seems, must be that I anticipate there being two horizons, two lives, both of which are mine,' says Jerome Valberg, continuing,

But this is not an experiential possibility. An experiential possibility is a way that things might develop from within my horizon (my life,

---

[4] [Aspects], in *Selected Prose*, p. 3.

consciousness, experience). But it is not a way things might develop from within my horizon that my horizon itself should double [... For] what could it be to anticipate the doubling of my horizon? As anticipated, the doubling would be anticipated as figuring within the same horizon as that from within which it is anticipated: my horizon. But if the anticipated doubling is the doubling of my horizon, this is incoherent.... In anticipating the doubling of my horizon, the oneness or unity of my horizon, the oneness of the very subject matter I anticipate doubling, is presupposed. [This] incoherence is not touched by introducing a novel way of counting persons, or by replacing questions about the identity of persons with questions about their survival. The doubling of my horizon does not make sense experientially.[5]

The upshot of this argument would seem to be that, even if we can treat persons as higher-order individuals, we cannot say the same about selves, the subjects of experience. It is an argument that Pessoa's highest stage of dreaming attempts to induce an experiential state that cannot exist, because, in trying to imagine *myself* as severally many selves at once, I seem to be trying to perform in imagination an act that presupposes the very unity it would deny (much as the attempt to doubt whether one is thinking is self-defeating because doubting is itself a form of thinking).

Perhaps one can respond by replying that the doubling of phenomenal horizons is not in fact a challenge to the supposed oneness of mine; it is rather that my consciousness now has a very particular structure, an added dimension, consisting in the crisscrossing or interweaving of two fields of experience, each of which preserves its own unity and wholeness. Pessoa introduces the term 'intersection' as a philosophical term of art precisely to denote the unified phenomenology of a doubled, interwoven experiential state. In one place he gives, as an example, the hypnagogic state:

We all know that most agreeable of mental states, when sleep is not yet cast off, and yet we have not yet awaked. The mind is still plunged into the dream it had in sleep, but it feels already around it the slow murmur and vague shadow of real things. This is the most natural state of intersected sensations; neither the subjective, nor the objective, consciousness being fully active, they seem to divide our mind between them, each inter-penetrating the other.[6]

[5] Valberg, J. J. *Dream, Death, and the Self.* Princeton, 2007, pp. 468–70.
[6] 'Technique of feeling' (15B³–14). A sketch in English. Cited in Pizarro, Jerónimo. 'Fernando Pessoa: Not one but many isms'. In Dix, Steffen, and Pizarro, Jerónimo, eds.,

In the hypnagogic state, according to contemporary accounts, we enter a liminal zone and 'experience the elements of dreams, without their coalescing into full-blown dream narratives. Sometimes we are still aware of our immediate surroundings and mental state; other times we're so completely absorbed in imagistic thought that the boundary between ourselves and what we're imagining seems to disappear.'[7] The fact that a loosening of the ego's boundaries is a key feature of the hypnagogic state is fascinating, because, as we have already seen and will see again below, depersonalization, the 'reduction of the personality to ashes', is for Pessoa the ultimate goal of the highest stage of dreaming.[8]

While the hypnagogic state occurs spontaneously, Pessoa claims that states of 'intersecting sensation' can also be brought about through the conscious exercise of guided attention. He refers to an ability he has acquired,

> to focus on various ideas at the same time, to observe certain things while at the same time dreaming other, very different things, to dream simultaneously of a real sunset over the real Tagus river and a dreamed morning on an inner Pacific Ocean; and the two dreamed things crisscross without blending, without anything getting mixed up beside the different emotional states induced by each. It's as if I saw a number of people walking down a street and felt all their souls inside me (which could occur only in a unity of feeling) at the same time that I saw their various bodies (these I could see only separately) crossing paths on the street full of legs in motion.[9]

To give literary shape to the results of his explorations in divided endogenous attention Pessoa experiments with an extreme form of poetry which he calls 'intersectionism', writing just six intersectionist poems collectively going by the name *Slanting Rain*. Pessoa claims that these poems capture the essence of the orthonym Fernando Pessoa:

> He will never produce anything that's more genuinely Fernando Pessoa. What could better express his relentlessly intellectualized sensibility, his

Portuguese Modernisms: Multiple Perspectives on Literature and the Visual Arts. Legenda, 2011, pp. 24–41, at p. 38.

[7] Thompson, Evan. *Waking, Dreaming, Being: Self and Consciousness in Neuroscience, Meditation and Philosophy.* Columbia, 2014, pp. 112–13.

[8] Another key feature of the hypnagogic state is synaesthesia, which Pessoa also claims to experience; *Selected Prose*, p. 67.

[9] 'Milky way', *The Book of Disquiet*, p. 435.

inattentively keen attention, and the ardent subtlety of his cold self-analysis than these poetic intersections in which the narrator's state of mind is simultaneously two states, in which the subjective and objective join together while remaining separate, and in which the real and the unreal merge in order to remain distinct? In these poems Fernando Pessoa made a veritable portrait of his soul. In that one, unique moment he succeeded in having his own individuality, such as he had never had before and can never have again, because he has no individuality.[10]

In these poems two subject positions are made to intersect by the crisscross-ing of distinct phenomenal fields, the implication being not that there is a successive switching from one viewpoint to another but that both fields are simultaneously available. Time is described as a 'twofold hour', while space is 'vertically horizontal'. In the first poem, the two fields of consciousness invoke those classic Pessoan tropes, a port and a landscape:

> My dream of an infinite port crosses this landscape
> And the flowers' colour is transparent to the sails of
>   large ships
> Casting off from the wharf, dragging the silhouettes of
>   these old
> Sunlit trees as their shadows over the waters...
>
> The port I dream of is somber and pallid,
> And the landscape is sunny viewed from this side...
> But in my mind today's sun is a somber port
> And the ships leaving the port are these sunlit trees...
>
> Freed into two, I slid straight down the landscape...
> The substance of the wharf is the clear and calm road
> That rises, going up like a wall,
> And the ships pass through the trunks of the trees
> In a vertically horizontal fashion,
> Dropping their lines in the water through the leaves one
>   by one...

---

[10] 'Notes for the memory of my master Caeiro', in *Selected Prose*, p. 50.

> I don't know who I dream I am...
> Suddenly all the seawater in the port is transparent
> And I see on the bottom, like a huge print unrolled
>   across it,
> This entire landscape, a row of trees, a road glowing in
>   that port,
> And the shadow of a sailing ship older than the port
>   and passing
> Between my dream of the port and my looking at this
>   landscape,
> And it approaches me, enters me,
> And passes to the other side of my soul...[11]

Pessoa, in this poem, is brilliantly trying to describe what it is like simultaneously to occupy two subject positions. There are two fields of experience here, one of a port, the other a landscape, and they are made to crisscross and intersect without ever merging or combining into one, as if the warp and weft of a woven fabric. Each has its own unity and wholeness, and each presents itself as all-inclusive. Their intersection is perhaps akin to that of a mixture, an emulsion of two liquids that do not chemically combine, an emulsion which nevertheless has a distinct colour of its own, a specific viscosity, and so on.

An intersectionist experience is one in which two discrete sensoria emulsify without synthesis, and for that reason permits us to say that there are two subject positions, which are nevertheless somehow constitutive of a unity. This is, of course, quite different from the idea that there may be two or more individuals at the perspectival centre of a single field of consciousness. For although it is in general the case that just one subject occupies the perspectival centre in a given field of perception, it is perfectly possible that there may be two or more. For a clear example, we have only to consider that famous painting, *Las Meninas,* by Velázquez. The perspectival centre is here occupied by the person whose image is reflected in a mirror at the back of the scene, the whole scene presented from the perspective that person occupies. Yet in fact there are two reflections in the mirror, those of Philip

---

[11] *A Little Larger,* p. 281. Pessoa's intersectionist poetry parallels the experiments in futurism of artists such as Santa-Rita Pintor, as in, for example, his 'Geometrical synthesis of a head x plastic infinite of atmosphere x physico-transcendentalism (Radiographic Sensibility)' (Paris 1913; published in *Orpheu*).

IV and his wife, Mariana of Austria. So the perspectival centre is, in the painting, doubly occupied. A scenario like this stands in stark contrast to what the doubled horizonality of intersectionist sensation strives for, an experience in which two discrete fields coexist in a single, emulsified unity. For another, startling example of the multiple occupation of a single subject position, consider the story in the *Mahābhārata* about the female philosopher Sulabhā. Wanting to talk with king Janaka, Sulabhā teleports herself to the palace, implants her mind into his soul, and the two of them engage in an internal dialogue![12] This thought experiment, astonishing as it is, vividly contrasts with the Pessoan wish 'to be two kings at the same time: not the one soul of them both, but two distinct, kingly souls,'[13] the simultaneous occupation of two perspectival centres rather than the dual occupation of a single one.

Pessoa describes the experience as consisting in 'dual attention':

> I've discovered that I'm always attentive to, and always thinking about, two things at the same time…Hunched over a ledger, I attentively record the entries that tell the useless history of an obscure firm, while at the same time and with equal attention my thoughts follow the route of a non-existent ship past landscapes of an unreal Orient. For me the two things are equally visible and equally distinct: the ruled pages on which I carefully write the commercial epic of Vasques & Co., and the deck where I carefully observe—beyond the ruled pattern of the floorboards' tarred joints—the rows of lounge chairs and the stretched legs of passengers relaxing on the voyage.[14]

Two fields of experience, each structured by attention, but kept from merging. Typically for Pessoa one field is external and the other internal, one 'objective' and the other 'subjective.'

Yet Pessoa abandoned his experiments in intersectionist poetry, and his view seems to have undergone a shift. I wonder if he recognized that the force of the idea behind simultaneous subject plurality, that is, the experiential possibility to be in multiple subject positions simultaneously yet severally, is not fully realized in the concept of an emulsified experience. There

---

[12] *Mahābhārata* 12.308. *The Mahābhārata*, translated by John Smith. Penguin Classics, 2009, p. 657.
[13] *The Book of Disquiet*, #404.   [14] *The Book of Disquiet*, #302.

seems to be an inherent tension in intersectionism: either the interwoven experience does indeed display a genuine phenomenological unity, in which case there is after all just one field of experience and just one subject position; or it remains divided into two, in which case it does nothing to demonstrate that there is indeed a genuine experiential possibility in play. A single, even if emulsified, field of experience requires just a single subject of experience: it does not exemplify the simultaneous experience of many subjects severally. While still believing in horizonal doubling as an experiential possibility, Pessoa's thought seems to have become that the use of the technique of 'double attention' has a primarily therapeutic value in bringing about depersonalization.

*　*　*

Reassembling all the elements we have thus far artificially separated, we can sum up by saying that Pessoa's philosophy of self consists in this, irreducibly first-personal, thesis: I am a single forum for the many subjects that I, successively and simultaneously, am. The enigmatic and apparently paradoxical status of this thesis remains to be resolved but, before turning to that large task in Part II, let me conclude here by adding more detail to my description of Pessoa's post-Cartesian philosophical methodology.

6

Simulating Subjectivity

'Due to my habit of dividing myself, following two distinct mental operations at the same time, it's generally the case that as I lucidly and intensely adapt myself to what others are feeling, I simultaneously under-take a rigorously objective analysis of their unknown self, what they think and are.'[1] Pessoa's technique of lucid analytical self-simulation comprises a new methodology in the philosophy of mind, one which I will call—in deliberate contrast to the empirical and transcendental phenomenology of his contemporary Edmund Husserl (1859–1938), of whose work he appears to have been unaware—an 'analytical phenomenology'.[2] The method con-sists in a meticulous, even 'scientific', introspective analysis of phenomenal experience: 'To reduce sensation to a science, to make psychological analysis into a microscopically precise method—that's the goal that occupies, like a steady thirst, the hub of my life's will.'[3] 'I believe that the future historian of his own sensations may be able to make a precise science out of the attitude he takes towards his self-awareness. We're only in the beginnings of this dif-ficult art—at this point just an art: the chemistry of sensations in its as yet alchemical stage. This scientist of tomorrow will pay special attention to his own inner life, subjecting it to analysis with a precision instrument created out of himself.'[4] Pessoa also speaks of '...the slow analysis of sensations,... used as an atomic science of the soul...'.[5]

As with all great philosophers, Pessoa crafts his own lexicon of philo-sophical terms. The lexicon includes 'sensation' (*sensação*), 'feeling' (*senti-mento*), 'dream' (*sonho*) and 'dreaming' (*sonhando*), 'landscape' (*paisagem*),

---

[1] *The Book of Disquiet*, #305.
[2] Pessoa's phenomenology has also been favourably contrasted with the existential phe-nomenology of Martin Heidegger (1889–1976): see Slaby, Jan. 'Living in the moment. Boredom and the meaning of existence in Heidegger and Pessoa'. *Yearbook for Eastern and Western Philosophy* (2) 2017, pp. 235–56; Marder, Michael. 'Phenomenology of distraction, or, attention in the fissuring of time and space'. *Research in Phenomenology* 41 (2011), pp. 396–419.
[3] 'Milky way', *The Book of Disquiet*, p. 431.   [4] *The Book of Disquiet*, #76.
[5] *The Book of Disquiet*, #155.

Virtual Subjects, Fugitive Selves: Fernando Pessoa and his Philosophy. Jonardon Ganeri,
Oxford University Press (2021). © Jonardon Ganeri.
DOI: 10.1093/oso/9780198864684.001.0001

'personality' (*personalidade*), 'soul' (*alma*), 'analysis' (*análise*), 'attention' (*atenção*), and 'intersection' (*intersecção*), as well as 'simulation' (*simulação*) and 'depersonalization' (despersonalização). The exact meaning of each of these terms needs to be understood from the contexts in which the term is used, and the uses to which it is put, rather than simply by consulting its dictionary definition. Pessoa's use of 'sensation' as a term of art has its origins in, and is carried over from, his early, pre-heteronymic, philosophical essays, where indeed he first develops a creed of sensationism. The scope of 'sensation' is there restricted to the deliverances of the five sense modalities: 'See, hear, smell, taste, feel—those are God's only commandments.'[6] Yet a Pessoan sensation is not a brute item of the sensorial given; it is not the basic response to stimulation of empirical psychology. What Pessoa means by 'sensation' is, rather, much closer to what contemporary philosophers mean when they talk about the phenomenal character of conscious perceptual experience: '[M]y sensations—states of conscious seeing, impressions gathered by intently hearing, and aromas through which the modesty of the outer world speaks to me of things from the past (so easily remembered by their smells), giving me a reality and an emotion that go beyond the simple fact of bread being baked inside the bakery.'[7] And the scope of 'sensation' soon comes to encompass the phenomenal character of sundry other psychological items—memories, hopes, and desires are explicitly included, not to mention pleasure and pain;[8] anxieties and other moods and emotions,[9] for which Pessoa sometimes uses the term 'feeling' (sometimes merely as a substitute for 'sensation'). If the heteronym Alberto Caeiro wants to eliminate from sensation any involvement of conceptual content, so as to experience things as directly and immediately as possible, what Bernardo Soares, the semi-heteronymic protagonist of *The Book of Disquiet,* realizes is that sensations are penetrated by cognition: 'Our sensations change according to how we understand them and to what extent.'[10] A Pessoan sensorium is thus a broad arena of phenomenal properties.

As indicated in the quotation with which I began this chapter, the method of an analytical phenomenology has two components. The first element is to simulate, in a guided or directed manner, a Pessoan sensorium. Pessoa has a

---

[6] 'Sensationism', in *Selected Prose,* p. 67.   [7] *The Book of Disquiet,* #208.
[8] *The Book of Disquiet,* #377.
[9] 'Sentimental education', in *The Book of Disquiet,* p. 455.
[10] *The Book of Disquiet,* #366. On the concept of cognitive penetration in philosophy and cognitive psychology, see Zeimbekis, John, and Raftopoulos, Athanassios, eds. *The Cognitive Penetrability of Perception: New Philosophical Perspectives.* Oxford, 2015.

technical term for such acts of simulation, 'dreaming', his use of the term not confined to actual dreaming but to the controlled and lucid simulation in wakeful consciousness of a sensorium. Pessoan 'dreaming' consists in the cultivation of sensations: 'For those who choose to make dreams their life, and to make a religion and politics out of cultivating sensations like plants in a hothouse...'[11]

Pessoan dreaming is an exercise of the imagination, whose cultivation, which Pessoa playfully describes as a 'sentimental education',[12] has two levels. One level consists simply in the use of imagination to know what it is like *oneself* to have an experience that one has not actually had: 'Dreamed pleasure is pleasure, albeit in a dream';[13] 'Conjectured feelings are what grieve and torment me, and the nostalgia that makes my eyes swell with tears is conceived and felt through imagination and projection';[14] 'I rejoice in imaginary breezes, but the imaginary lives while it's being imagined.'[15] We might articulate this as a principle about imagination: having an experience is not the only way to know what it is like to have it; imagining a sensation is also a way to access its phenomenal character. At this level, the role of the imagination is simply to broaden and deepen one's actual sensorium, not to simulate a new one. As Pessoa puts it,

to be able to convert our interior vision, the hearing of our dreams, and all imagined senses and the senses of the imagination into tangible receptors like the five senses that receive the outside world: these are some of the sensations (and similar examples can be imagined) that the trained cultivator of his own feelings is able to experience with a convulsive fervour.[16]

A second level involves my use of imagination to know what it is like for *someone else* (or rather, another I) to have an experience. Assuming a heteronym is an act of imagination at this more nuanced level, a level at which imagination consists in the simulation of a Pessoan sensorium. Imagination is a mode of phenomenal access in the sense that it not only enables me to know what it is like *for me* to see a certain sunset; it enables me to know what it is like *for you* (for another I) to see the sunset. It is here that the concept of heteronymic simulation is crucial. A heteronym is a virtual subject, a subject of perceptual experience, emotion, and thought which is

---

[11] 'Sentimental education', *The Book of Disquiet*, p. 453.
[12] 'Sentimental education', *The Book of Disquiet*, pp. 453–7.   [13] *A Little Larger*, p. 119.
[14] *The Book of Disquiet*, #266.   [15] *The Book of Disquiet*, #378.
[16] 'Sentimental education', *The Book of Disquiet*, pp. 453–4.

simulated in imagination. What I do when I imagine what it is like for you to see the sunset is that I heteronymically simulate you; I imagine myself as you, seeing the sunset. Imagining how it is for S to feel something is a matter of assuming the heteronym S and, as S, having that feeling. Pessoa illustrates the technique as applied to the simulation of another's pain:

> First we must create another I, charged with suffering—in and for us—everything we suffer. Next we need to create an inner sadism, completely masochistic, that enjoys its suffering as if it were someone else's...[W]hen every felt pain (felt so quickly there's no time for the soul to plan any defence) is automatically analysed to the core, foisted on an extraneous I, and buried in me to the utmost height of pain, then I truly feel like a victor....[17]

This is the use of imagination in heteronymic simulation, and Pessoa further describes it thus: 'I dream myself and choose those parts of me that are dreamable, constructing and reconstructing myself in every way possible until what I am and what I am not conform to my ideal.'[18]

Pessoa's invention of the heteronym is thus motivated by a keen awareness of the existence of limits on the experience of any single individual. There are spatio-temporal constraints on what any finite being can experience, simply because an embodied human being cannot be everywhere and see or feel everything. What one cannot experience at first hand, however, one can imagine, and imagination therefore has the power to ameliorate the frustrations of our empirical bounds. In imagination, Pessoa claims, I can come to know what it would be like for me to undergo experiences I have not had. It is basic to Pessoa's project that imagining having an experience, which is what Pessoa means by his term of art 'dreaming', is a form of access to the phenomenal character of the experience imagined.

The Pessoan concept of 'dreaming' is closely related to what has more recently been called 'enactive imagination'. Alvin Goldman makes the concept central in his book *Simulating Minds*. He says,

> I can imagine seeing a yellow parrot, feeling sad, feeling outraged, or feeling elated. It is also possible, no doubt, to imagine that one feels elated, which is equivalent to assuming the truth of the proposition 'I am elated'.

---

[17] 'Sentimental education', in *The Book of Disquiet*, p. 455.
[18] 'Milky way', *The Book of Disquiet*, p. 434.

But there is another way to imagine feeling elated, namely, to conjure up a state that feels, phenomenologically, rather like a trace or tincture of elation. Our ability to do this is not confined to sensations, perceptions, or emotions. One can also imagine having attitudes such as desire, hope, doubt, and ambivalence. The range of states that can be imagined suggests that imagining, in a more inclusive sense, is an operation or process capable of creating a wide variety of mental states .... When I imagine feeling elated, I do not merely suppose that I am elated; rather, I enact, or try to enact, elation itself. Thus, we might call this type of imagination 'enactive imagination'.[19]

The critical feature of enactive imagination is that the imagined state resembles its target, and so is a way to understand the minds of others, to mindread:

If enactive imagining is utilized for mindreading, and if its mindreading applications are to be accurate (i.e., yield correct imputations), it seems necessary that outputs of enactive imagination should resemble their counterparts in important respects. Is such resemblance psychologically feasible? Can 'endogenously' produced mental states resemble those that are produced in a normal, 'exogenous' fashion? ... How similar is enactively imagined desire-that-p to genuine desire-that-p? How similar is enactively imagined belief-that-p to genuine belief-that-p?[20]

Carefully reviewing the limited empirical research on this question, Goldman identifies a body of research on two types of enactive imagination, visual and motor enactive imagination, normally described as visual and motor 'imagery'. He finds that

psychology and neuroscience have revealed extensive and often surprising correspondences between visual imagery and perception. This suggests that the power of enactive imagination is very considerable, at least in the visual domain.... The case for similarity between motor imagery and its counterpart is, if anything, stronger than the one for visual imagery, though less well known or introspectively compelling.[21]

---

[19] Goldman, Alvin. *Simulating Minds: The Philosophy, Psychology and Neuroscience of Mindreading*. Oxford, 2006, p.47.

[20] Goldman, *Simulating Minds*, pp. 149, 151.

[21] Goldman, *Simulating Minds*, pp. 151, 157.

Goldman's conclusion is very conducive to Pessoa's project: it is that 'enactive imagination is a robust phenomenon, capable of producing outputs that correspond closely to counterpart states'.[22] Naturally, the correspondence that is of interest to Pessoa is a correspondence at the level of the phenomenology, and his claim about what he calls 'dreaming' (enactive imagination) is that the 'sensations' (imagery) that constitute a Pessoan sensorium either closely resemble actual counterparts or else are actually identical to fictitious ones.[23]

Pessoan 'dreaming' is a method for obtaining knowledge, because heteronymic simulation puts one in contact with features of reality that cannot be understood otherwise: 'Only the eyes we use for dreaming truly see'.[24] Pessoa does also sometimes describe the creative exercise of the imagination as spontaneous and exogenous, most strikingly in his account of the 'triumphal day' in which his three principal heteronyms appeared to him in a single moment of inspiration, and during which he claims to have composed more than thirty poems including all six intersectionist poems. There is no question but that this is a piece of autobiographical fictionalization, and yet Pessoa is making an important point about the creative process. He talks of being 'possessed' as if by a spirit in such occasions, talk which, as we have seen, should not be confused with the sort of involuntariness that is associated with mental disorder, a hallmark of mental disorder being that one cannot escape the disordered state by an exercise of will. The point is rather that creative inspiration is akin to being in what is known as the 'flow': absorbed, engaged, involved, 'automatic' even, but, nevertheless, the skilled activity of someone who is an expert in what they do.

---

[22] Goldman, *Simulating Minds*, p. 158.
[23] I will say more about this in the chapter 'The Reality of Subjects' below.
[24] *The Book of Disquiet*, #123. Pessoan 'dreaming' is what the Indians call a *pramāṇa*.

7

Analytical Attention

The second element in Pessoa's philosophical method is that of impartial analysis: 'On a tram in motion I'm able, through my constant and instantaneous analysis, to separate the idea of the tram from the idea of speed, separating them so completely that they're distinct things-in-reality. Then I can feel myself riding not inside the tram but inside its Mere Speed.'[1] Again, 'Taking the dress of the girl in front of me, I break it down into the fabric from which it's made and the work that went into making it (such that I see a dress and not just fabric), and the delicate embroidery that trims the collar decomposes under my scrutiny into the silk thread with which it was embroidered and the work it took to embroider it.'[2] Pessoa regards such analytical observation as a mode of attention: 'This scientist of tomorrow will pay special attention to his own inner life, subjecting it to analysis with a precision instrument created out of himself.'[3]

Pessoa's technique of deliberately guiding the attention to one's own experience, and, specifically, to the outputs of 'dreaming' or enactive imagination, has a modern echo in the psychological technique of descriptive experience sampling. In this technique a beeper is used randomly to cue subjects to give their attention to their experience at the moment they hear the beep. They are then instructed to record in a notebook the features of the experience at that particular moment. They are also made to describe it in an in-depth interview conducted shortly afterwards, the interviewer asking just one question: 'What was occurring in your inner experience at the moment of the beep?'[4] What the experiments find is that interviewees are often unaware of their thoughts until they become targets of descriptive experience sampling. One natural conclusion we can draw is that subjects are not immediately aware of the contents of their own minds, but rather that introspective self-awareness requires that one's attention is guided to

---

[1] *The Book of Disquiet*, #75.   [2] *The Book of Disquiet*, #298.
[3] *The Book of Disquiet*, #76.
[4] Hurlburt, Russell, and Akhter, Sarah. 'The descriptive experience sampling method'. *Phenomenology and the Cognitive Sciences* 5 (2006), pp. 271–301.

Virtual Subjects, Fugitive Selves: Fernando Pessoa and his Philosophy. Jonardon Ganeri,
Oxford University Press (2021). © Jonardon Ganeri.
DOI: 10.1093/oso/9780198864684.001.0001

the contents of one's inner experience. Pessoa is passionate about recording the landscape of those inner worlds which he himself, in guided simulation, brings into being. Or, as he puts it so much better himself, 'I know nothing greater, nor more worthy of the truly great man, than the patient and expressive analysis of the ways in which we don't know ourselves, the conscious recording of the unconsciousness of our conscious states, the metaphysics of autonomous shadows, the poetry of the twilight of disillusion.'[5] Pessoan analysis is a sort of ongoing and self-cued application of descriptive experience sampling, directed less at the intentional content of one's thoughts as at the phenomenal character of one's experience.

Pessoa's description of an analytical attention to one's own mental state might be held to constitute a theory of introspection. It is one which, while claiming that introspection is grounded in attention, also emphasizes the idea that introspection transforms the state of which one becomes aware, for example by intensifying, enriching, and sharpening it: 'Our sensations change according to how we understand them.'[6] Analytical attention, Pessoa says, 'shapes' the phenomenal character of a sensation: 'This step...is to immediately pass the sensation through pure intelligence, filtering it through a higher analysis that shapes it into a literary form with its own substance and character.'[7] Several contemporary theorists of introspection have agreed that introspection is attention-based,[8] and there is a growing acknowledgement that it is a type of attention under which the sensation is itself potentially transformed. Christopher Hill employs the term 'introspective attention'[9] and he argues that introspective attention cannot be reduced to inner perception: the model of introspection as inner perception cannot survive the observation that introspective attention is transformative. Hill writes,

There has been little recognition of the fact that a sensation may be transformed by the act of coming to attend to it, and even less of the fact that a sensation may be brought into existence by attention. Instead of facing these facts and attempting to explain them, philosophers have often waged an imperialist struggle on behalf of inner vision and the inner eye

---

[5] *The Book of Disquiet*, #149.   [6] *The Book of Disquiet*, #336.
[7] 'Sentimental education', in *The Book of Disquiet*, p. 456.
[8] Lycan, William. 'The superiority of HOP to HOT'. In Rocco J. Gennaro, ed., *Higher-Order Theories of Consciousness*. John Benhamins, 2004, pp. 93–114; Wu, Wayne. 'Introspection as Attention and Action' (forthcoming); my *Attention, Not Self*. Oxford, 2017, pp. 230–2.
[9] Hill, Christopher. *Consciousness*. Cambridge, 2009, p. 235.

hypothesis....I see no reason to prefer imperialism to the view that the phenomenal field is often profoundly changed by the process of coming to attend to a sensation....Thus, consider a case in which someone decides to focus on a sensation that has heretofore been at the margin of consciousness. If the sensation is an itch, attending to it may make it more importunate; if it is a pain, attending to it may make it more severe; if it is an auditory sensation, attending to it may increase its phenomenal volume; if it is a visual sensation, attending to it may increase its vividness; and so on.[10]

The point which is most relevant to Pessoa's analytical phenomenology is that introspective attention ('analysis') and enactive simulation ('dreaming') work together in tandem, feeding back on each other, rather than existing as entirely separable operations.

There is a clear correlation between the two components in an analytical phenomenology and the two principles which are fundamental to Pessoa's philosophy of self. Simulation is the principle that I am able to occupy the subject position in fields of experience other than this one. Depersonalization is the principle that there is a type of self-consciousness consisting in attention to the field thus occupied. When Pessoa imagines what it is like to be a fly,[11] he imagines himself as a fly ('I really felt like a fly when I imagined I felt like one. And I felt I had a flyish soul, slept flyishly and was flyishly withdrawn'), thereby simulating a flyish field of sensation with himself, qua fly, at the centre, and he simultaneously and interactively attends to the simulated experience ('I looked at it from the depths of the abyss, anonymous and attentive'). One is the process by which the phenomenal field is constituted and woven; the other is a process of detached analysis: 'To live is to crochet according to a pattern we were given. But while doing it the mind

---

[10] Hill, Christopher. *Sensations: A Defence of Type Materialism*. Cambridge, 1991, pp. 123–5. The same point is made by Hubert Dreyfus in his review of *The Embodied Mind*, a book which has been very influential in the subsequent rise of the 'contemplative science' movement. Dreyfus argues that the book struggles in its 'attempt to reconcile transformation and discovery'. Dreyfus, Hubert, 'Review of *The Embodied Mind*'. *Mind* 102 (1993), pp. 542–6, at p. 544. While describing his method as a science, Pessoa regards the transformative nature of introspective attention as an essential methodological feature, and his discoveries are precisely about the transformative effects of imaginative simulation and introspective attention. Varela, Francisco, Thompson, Evan, and Rosch, Eleanor. *The Embodied Mind: Cognitive Science and Human Experience*. MIT Press, 1991. See Evan Thompson's introduction to the revised 2016 edition for a discussion of Dreyfus's review.

[11] *The Book of Disquiet*, #334. I will say more about the 'fly' passage below.

is at liberty, and all enchanted princes can stroll in their parks between one and another plunge of the hooked ivory needle.'[12]

Pessoa's methodology for the study of the mind consists in an interactive interplay between enactive imagination and introspective attention. The use of these instruments together makes it possible to simulate in a first-personal fashion a field of experience and to analyse its contents and structure. One turns oneself into a putative other and at the same time closely attends to what it is like. Pessoa calls these the 'two realities' that are constitutive of an analytical phenomenology:

> The man of science realizes that the only reality for him is his own self, and that the only real world is the world as his sensations give it to him. That's why, instead of following the fallacious path of adapting his sensations to other people's, he uses objective science to try to achieve a perfect knowledge of his world and his personality. There's nothing more objective than his dreams, and nothing more infallibly his than his self-awareness. Around these two realities he refines his science.[13]

In using the language of scientific objectivity, Pessoa is evidently being somewhat tongue-in-cheek, but his serious point is that subjective experience is no less 'real' than is the physical world.

The analytical phenomenologist is, for Pessoa, a fusion of the poet and the dramatist, and in a letter to a friend he describes himself as first and foremost a dramatic poet:

> The central point of my personality as an artist is that I'm a dramatic poet; in everything I write, I always have the poet's inner exaltation and the playwright's depersonalization. I soar as someone else—that's all...[The critic] knows that as a poet I feel; that as a dramatic poet I feel with complete detachment from my feeling self; that as a dramatist (without the poet) I automatically transform what I feel into an expression far removed from what I felt, and I create, in my emotions, a nonexistent person who truly felt that feeling and, in feeling it, felt yet other, related emotions that I, purely I, forgot to feel.[14]

Heteronymy is the transformation of oneself into another I, a virtual self (a 'non-existent person') whose landscape of sensation is simulated by the poet

---

[12] The Book of Disquiet, #12.   [13] 'Milky way', The Book of Disquiet, p. 431.
[14] Letter to João Gaspar Simões, 11 December 1931, Selected Prose, p. 246.

and attended to by the playwright. There is more than an echo in this of Nietzsche's account of drama in *The Birth of Tragedy*: 'This process of the tragic chorus is the original *dramatic* phenomenon: to see oneself transformed before one's very eyes and now to act as if one had really entered into another body and another character.'[15] As for who Pessoa means by the one who is 'purely I', surely this can refer only to the forum, to that impersonal sort of self-awareness in which one thinks of oneself as a harbour and a meeting place, a place from which one can analyse the inner lives of the heteronyms.

Let me, finally, consider two sorts of challenge to Pessoa's analytical phenomenology. An analytical phenomenology consists in two elements, enactive imagination (that is, 'simulation') and analytical attention (elsewhere called 'depersonalization'). Someone might argue that these two elements are in fact incompatible with one another, and do so by pointing to the phenomenon of choking. Choking is what happens to sports players when instead of simply allowing themselves to be absorbed in playing the shot they focus their attention on what they are doing, something that often leads to a serious diminution in the level of performance. While choking has to do with the skilful performance of a physical activity, there are surely parallels in the activity of immersing oneself within a phenomenological landscape. Can one really appreciate a piece of music if one is, at the same time as listening to it, also engaging in an analytical scrutiny of every note?

And yet the evidence is not nearly as clear as these examples might suggest. For, as the ballerina-turned-philosopher Barbara Montero shows in her book *Thought in Action: Expertise and the Conscious Mind*,[16] it is actually a myth that thinking about what you are doing always hinders performance. She argues for a view of expertise in which expert action is in general thoughtful and reflective: a ballerina is, and has to be, intensely aware of her every movement even as she makes it. Pessoan phenomenology says that we should strive to become experts in the art of enactive imagination, and experts in exactly Montero's sense, fully reflective and thoughtful about our imaginative actions even as we perform them. This is, perhaps, what he means by 'the art of effective dreaming for metaphysical minds.'[17]

---

[15] Nietzsche, Friedrich. *The Birth of Tragedy*, translated by Douglas Smith. Oxford, 2008, p. 50.

[16] Montero, Barbara. *Thought in Action: Expertise and the Conscious Mind*. Oxford, 2016.

[17] 'The art of effective dreaming (I)', *The Book of Disquiet*, p. 400.

A different sort of threat to analytical phenomenology comes in the form of a challenge to its basic principle, that imagining having an experience is a mode of phenomenal access. There is a general presumption in contemporary philosophy of mind, reinforced by such classic thought experiments as the so-called knowledge argument,[18] that the only way to know what it is like to have an experience, say of seeing the colour blue, is by having the experience itself, actually seeing blue. As David Lewis summarizes the import of the knowledge argument, 'If you want to know what some new and different experience is like, you can learn it by going out and really having that experience. You can't learn it by being told about the experience, however thorough your lessons may be.'[19] Still Lewis only says 'can', not 'must', and so this is at least formally compatible with the Pessoan claim that enactive imagination is another way to know what a new experience is like without going out and really having it. Indeed, Lewis himself concedes that there could be other ways to learn what experiences are like:

Having an experience is surely one good way, and surely the only practical way, of coming to know what that experience is like. Can we say, flatly, that it is the only possible way? Probably not. There is a change that takes place in you when you have the experience and thereby come to know what it's like. Perhaps the exact same change could in principle be produced in you by precise neurosurgery, very far beyond the limits of present-day technique. Or it could possibly be produced in you by magic.[20]

The challenge to analytical phenomenology comes in the shape of an argument that there is a special type of experience such that you *must* go out and really have it in order to know what having it is like. This is what Laurie Paul claims in her book *Transformative Experience*.[21] Paul says,

If becoming a vampire was not a radically new kind of experience for you, you could simulate forward by, in a sense, mentally putting yourself in the shoes of the person who had become a vampire and evaluating the outcome from that perspective. But since you don't know how the change will be wrought in you (because you don't know what it will be like to become

[18] Jackson, Frank. 'What Mary didn't know'. *The Journal of Philosophy* 83 (1986), pp. 291–5.
[19] Lewis, David. 'What experience teaches'. *Proceedings of the Russellian Society* 13 (1988), pp. 29–50, at p. 29.
[20] Lewis, 'What experience teaches', p. 29.
[21] Paul, Laurie. *Transformative Experience*. Oxford, 2014.

a vampire), you don't know which new core preferences you'll have. In other words, you won't know whose shoes to mentally step into to assess the values of the post-change outcome.[22]

Her argument is that these types of experience, for which she prescriptively reserves the label 'transformative experience', are such that the difference between the pre-experience and the post-experience self is so great that enactive imagination cannot put you in a position to assess, prior to the experience, what subjective value your post-experience self will put on the experiential state it finds itself in.

Yet Pessoa's great discovery is that the imagination has two levels, and it is only if one fails to appreciate this that Paul's argument goes through. The first level is to use the imagination to expand one's own sensorium, and so used imagination evidently cannot transform oneself into another. The second level is that of heteronymic simulation, enactive imagination, and it is Pessoa's entire point that the exercise of the imagination at this second level is indeed transformative. It is by way of enactive imagination that I can say, 'I'm someone else in the way I'm I.' If Pessoa is right then self-transformation does not, contra Paul, require that one undergoes what she calls a 'transformative experience', such as actually becoming a vampire (or, another of Paul's examples, a mother, etc.). The very idea that it is possible to assume a heteronym entails that this is not the only way to undergo a change of self. Pessoa, the poet, sees more potential in the imagination than does the philosopher, Paul. He sees that imagination itself affords a route to self-transformation, for in heteronymic simulation one does undergo a change of self, albeit a controlled and reversible change: 'To understand what someone feels is to be him.'[23] So the reply to this objection is that once we have available to us the distinction between two stages of imagination and hence to the idea of heteronymic simulation, we can see that—at least for someone whose powers of imagination afford them a capacity for heteronymic simulation, and it is Pessoa's view that we can all so 'educate our sentiments'— there are no transformative experiences in Paul's technical sense, experiences that engender transformations of self such that one *cannot* know what it is like to be in the transformed state without actually having the experience.

---

[22] Paul. *Transformative Experience*, p. 116.   [23] 'Sensationism', *Selected Prose*, p. 67.

Given the capacity of the imagination to extend the reach of our access within the domain of the phenomenal, it is conceivable that someone might take as a regulative ideal in life the ambition to experience everything in every way: 'Since every noble soul desires to live life in its entirety—experiencing all things, all places and all feelings—and since this is objectively impossible, the only way for a noble soul to live life is subjectively; only by denying life can it be lived in its totality.'[24] It is in *Time's Passage*, a poem by the exuberant and life-loving Campos, that the idea is most vividly expressed:

> To feel everything in every way,
> To live everything from all sides,
> To be the same thing in all ways possible at the same time,
> To realize in oneself all humanity at all moments
> In one scattered, extravagant, complete, and aloof moment.[25]

As an ideal, something whose function is regulate the way one lives rather than a state anyone expects actually to achieve, this does indeed capture something of the spirit of the heteronym Campos. The ideal that regulates the life of Caeiro is a different one, to live in as immediate and direct a way as possible, and of Reis to live with classical refinement.

Pessoa seems eventually to have regarded the various stratagems available in order 'to feel everything in every way' as techniques whose ultimate goal is the reduction of the personality to ashes, which, in an insightfully taxonomic remark that recapitulates much of our discussion, he says can come about '...by the acceptance in one and the same individual of all possible modes of feeling and thinking, even though incompatible with one another, whether they are felt simultaneously (psychic intersectionism), successively (sensationist dynamism), or separately, as if with different souls (polypersonality).'[26] He seems here to acknowledge that simultaneous subject plurality (his 'polypersonality') is not fully realized in the idea of intersectional experience. Pessoa's discovery is that there is something which

---

[24] *The Book of Disquiet*, #232.   [25] *Fernando Pessoa & Co.: Selected Poems*, p. 146.
[26] Pizarro, Jerónimo, ed., *Sensacionismo e Outros Ismos*, volume x of the critical edition of Fernando Pessoa. Imprensa Nacional-Casa da Moeda, 2009, p. 240. Cited in Pizarro, Jerónimo. 'Fernando Pessoa: Not one but many isms'. In Dix, Steffen, and Pizarro, Jerónimo, eds. *Portuguese Modernisms: Multiple Perspectives on Literature and the Visual Arts*. Legenda, 2011, pp. 24–41, at p. 35.

cannot be personified, rather an irony for the inventor of heteronymy and someone whose name means 'person'. He has devised a new *askesis*, a set of techniques whose aim is to make us aware of the non-personal behind the personal, to bring into view something present but hidden from light. The simulation of a multiplicity of heteronyms is one such technique, the analytical attention to the sensorium another. What is thereby made manifest is the forum, a form of self-awareness hidden within each of us, largely overlooked by the philosophers but intimately understood by the poets.

PART II
PESSOA PARAPHRASED

8

The Grammar of Subjectivity

It is within the biological human being that heteronymic states of mind occur. What we have to do is understand the rather complex grammar of such a state, as it is occurring in a person and supervening on the state of their body and brain. How are we to analyse the logical form of the conscious state of mind Pessoa is in when, assuming the heteronym Alberto Caeiro, he enactively imagines himself seeing a stone?

There is a commonly agreed way to articulate the logical form of a conscious state: it a state such that there is something it is like for a subject to be in it.[1] This formula has the important virtue that it enables us to separate out two distinct aspects in the phenomenology of an experience: *what* is experienced, the 'quality' of the experience; and *how* it is experienced, that it is experienced as being for-a-subject. Phenomenality has therefore been said to occur along two experiential dimensions:

> There are two important dimensions to my having this reddish experience. First...there is something it's like for me to have this experience....Being an experience, its being reddish is 'for me', a way it's like *for me*, in a way that being red is like nothing for—in fact is not in any way 'for'—my diskette case. Let's call this the subjectivity of conscious experience....The second important dimension of experience that requires explanation is qualitative character itself. Subjectivity is the phenomenon of there being something it's like for me to see the red diskette case. Qualitative character concerns the 'what' it's like for me: reddish or greenish, painful or pleasurable, and the like.[2]

The two dimensions are, thus, those of *qualitative* and *subjective* character.

Just what is the 'for-me-ness' that constitutes the subjective dimension of phenomenal character? On a deflationary interpretation there is nothing

---

[1] Nagel, Thomas. 'What is it like to be a bat?' *The Philosophical Review* 83.4 (1974), pp. 435–50.
[2] Levine, Joseph. *Purple Haze: The Puzzle of Consciousness.* Oxford, 2001, p. 7.

Virtual Subjects, Fugitive Selves: Fernando Pessoa and his Philosophy. Jonardon Ganeri,
Oxford University Press (2021). © Jonardon Ganeri.
DOI: 10.1093/oso/9780198864684.001.0001

more to an experience being for-me than that it is 'in' me, that it belongs to my mental life or stream of experience. Yet the point of describing it as a dimension of phenomenality is to resist a deflationary interpretation in favour of an experiential construal, according to which being-for-me is a fact about the phenomenology, about the manner in which experience is given. As Joseph Levine puts it, 'The very phrase that serves to canonically express the notion of the phenomenal—"what it's like for *x* to..."—explicitly refers to the phenomenal state being "for" the subject...Phenomenal states/ properties are not merely instantiated in the subject, but are experienced by the subject.'[3] In the elegant phrase Dan Zahavi introduces in his book *Self and Other*, being for-me is the 'dative of manifestation', a phenomenal feature that persists through the plurality of changing experiences.[4] It is, he says, a 'first-personal mode of givenness' and is that in virtue of which experience is 'lived through' by me and not merely occurrent within me. So for-me-ness is said to be 'an invariant dimension of phenomenal character [...and...] the categorical basis of our capacity for first-person thought'.[5]

Pessoa, naturally, is completely familiar with this distinction between two dimensions of phenomenality. He already anticipates the distinction in this passage:

The only way you can have new sensations is by forging a new soul. It's useless to try to feel new things without feeling them in a new way, and you can't feel in a new way without changing your soul. For things are what we feel they are—how long have you known this without yet knowing it?—and the only way for there to be new things, for us to feel new things, is for there to be some novelty in how we feel them.[6]

Pessoa's terms are 'feeling' (*sentimento*) and 'sensation' (*sensação*), and in speaking about feelings or sensations he is referring to what we are now calling the qualitative dimension of experience. He also, however, introduces a notion of 'how things feel' (*senti-las*) or a 'way' (*maneira*) of feeling. One might be tempted to read these phrases too as simply indicative of

---

[3] Levine, Joseph. 'Two kinds of access'. *Behavioral and Brain Sciences* 30 (2007), pp. 514–15, at p. 514.
[4] Zahavi, Dan. *Self and Other: Exploring Subjectivity, Empathy, and Shame*. Oxford, 2015, p. 19.
[5] Zahavi, Dan, and Kriegel, Uriah. 'For-me-ness: What it is and what it is not'. In Daniel O. Dahlstrom, Andreas Elpidorou, and Walter Hopp (eds.), *Philosophy of Mind and Phenomenology: Conceptual and Empirical Approaches*. Routledge, 2015, p. 49.
[6] *The Book of Disquiet*, #301.

qualitative character. For, indeed, the nearest equivalent in many languages of the English construction 'what is it like' is 'how is it', and in fact the Portuguese translator of Nagel's paper 'What is it like to be a bat?' renders the title as '*Como é ser um morcego?*' [How is it to be a bat?]. Yet in this passage his principal claim is that there can be no change in 'how things feel' without a change of what he refers to simply as 'soul' (*alma*), and that is sufficient to establish that it is really the dative of manifestation, the for-me-ness of experience, that he has in mind. It is clear that what Pessoa is speaking about is not the difference between how a red experience is as contrasted with a blue experience but how my experience is as contrasted with yours, that is to a comparatively fixed and 'invariant' dimension in felt experience. Contemporary philosophy has a specific term for the dependence relation in question, namely 'supervenience'—X supervenes on Y if there can be no change in X without a change in Y—and Pessoa's more specific claim is that the howness of experience supervenes on whatever it is he means by 'soul'.

It is evident from another passage that Pessoa does not think of 'soul' as a metaphysical substance but as a psychological achievement. He says:

> If I want to say I exist, I'll say 'I am'. If I want to say I exist as a separate entity, I'll say, 'I am myself'. But if I want to say I exist as an entity that addresses and acts on itself, exercising the divine function of self-creation, then I'll make *to be* into a transitive verb. Triumphantly and anti-grammatically supreme, I'll speak of 'amming myself'. I'll have stated a philosophy in just two words.[7]

The idea that the self consists in, or is the result of, an act of self-creation is again echoed here: 'I dream myself and choose those parts of me that are dreamable, constructing and reconstructing myself in every way possible until what I am and what I am not conform to my ideal.'[8]

As a term of art in Pessoa's philosophy, then, 'soul' (*alma*) refers to (the outcome of) self-constitutive processes of addressing and acting on oneself. The relationship is explored again in still another passage:

> The most that I've loved are my sensations—states of conscious seeing, impressions gathered by intently hearing, and aromas through which the

---

[7] *The Book of Disquiet*, #84.
[8] 'Milky way', *The Book of Disquiet*, p. 434. See also my 'Self as performance', in *The Concealed Art of the Soul*. Oxford, 2007, ch. 7.

modesty of the outer world speaks to me of things from the past... This is my morality, or metaphysics, or me: passer-by of everything, even of my own soul, I belong to nothing, I desire nothing, I am nothing — just an abstract centre of impersonal sensations, a fallen sentient mirror reflecting the world's diversity.[9]

A Pessoan sensation is a state of conscious seeing, not merely a sense-datum or stimulus. What this passage adds is the new thought that the process of 'amming' achieves the alignment of experience with respect to a centre. So, finally, Pessoa's view is that ways of feeling supervene on the centres with respect to which experience is aligned.

Notice, now, that the phrase 'the subject' is used twice over by Levine when he says that phenomenal states 'are not merely instantiated in the subject, but are experienced by the subject'.[10] What Pessoa's discovery of the heteronym alerts us to is that there is no guarantee that these two occurrences of the same phrase do in fact corefer. For in the case in which Pessoa assumes the heteronym Caeiro and writes poetry as Caeiro, it is certainly *in Pessoa* that the phenomenal states are instantiated; recall that he says of the heteronyms that 'they erupt inside me, where only I experience them'. Yet we now want to be able to say that it is *by Caeiro* that the phenomenal state is experienced, that the 'I' in 'only I experience them', the experiencing subject, is, for example, Caeiro. Then we can say of the famous lines, 'Countless lives inhabit us / I don't know, when I think or feel / Who it is that thinks or feels', that the one who doesn't know is the subject in whom the thinking and feeling is instantiated, and what is called into doubt is the identity of the subject who it is that is thinking and feeling, the subject by whom these things are experienced. One might say, as famously did Paul in his *Epistle to the Galatians*, 'It is no longer I, but Christ who lives in me',[11] frankly reporting a lived experience which was in-Paul but by-Christ. 'Each of my dreams', says Pessoa, 'as soon as I start dreaming it, is immediately incarnated in another person, who is then the one dreaming it, and not I',[12] the first person referring to the subject in whom the dream occurs, and this is not the same as the subject by whom it is experienced, the other person in whom it

---

[9] *The Book of Disquiet*, #84.   [10] 'Two kinds of access', p. 514.
[11] Galatians 2:20. *The Holy Bible: English Standard Version*. American Bible Society, 2004, p. 826.
[12] *The Book of Disquiet*, #299.

is incarnated. 'Each of us is two,' he says, 'the man who dreams in the man who acts....'[13]

A careful examination of the syntax of the 'what it's like...' construction, in English at least, reveals that it sustains still another distinction. One implicit argument place is generated by the presence of an infinitive verb. A verb phrase such as 'to write a poem' requires a covert subject (which linguists call 'PRO'), and which is filled in by using the prepositional phrase 'for S'. So linguists say that the sentence 'There is something it takes to write a poem' has the grammatical form 'There is something it takes for S_i [PRO_i to write a poem]'. A second implicit argument place is generated by the finite clause 'it is like..', which introduces, straightforwardly, a place for the subject of the finite verb. Daniel Stoljar stresses this distinction in the course of a probing analysis of the grammar of the construction. He offers this mundane example to illustrate the point:

> Suppose Bill is a very strange person who reacts in an odd way when he is in the presence of someone else (Alice, say) eating a peach. What happens is that he is overcome with an intense feeling of anger and also suffers an outbreak of prickly hives. In that case we might say 'There is something it is like to Bill for Alice to eat a peach'. Here it is intuitively Bill who is the subject of the experience, but it is not Bill but Alice who is the intended subject of the infinitive verb.[14]

So the sentence 'There is something it is like to experience a toothache' has the complete grammatical form, 'There is something it is like to x for y to experience a toothache.' The to-S position designates 'the psychological subject', that is, 'who it is that is affected by the state'.[15] The for-S position designates 'the intended subject' of the infinitive verb, that is, 'who the subject of the relevant state is'.[16]

It is easy to overlook this distinction because grammatical conventions of coreference apply when one or other position is unvoiced. In particular, if neither is voiced, coreference is required: the subject of the toothache and the subject of the experience must be identical.[17] Stoljar argues that the

---

[13] 'The river of possession', *The Book of Disquiet*, p. 448.
[14] Stoljar, Daniel. 'The semantics of 'what it's like' and the nature of consciousness'. *Mind* 125 (2016), pp. 1161–98.
[15] Stoljar, 'The semantics of 'what it's like', p. 1194.
[16] Stoljar, 'The semantics of 'what it's like', p. 1194.
[17] Stoljar, 'The semantics of 'what it's like', p. 1169.

'what is it like' construction, which, as I have noted, is in many languages, including Portuguese, rendered more naturally in a 'how'-locution such as 'How is it to be?', introduces a quantification over ways. So his final analysis of the logical form of 'There is something it is like to have a toothache' is as the three-place relation 'There is some way it is to x for y to have a toothache',[18] which can usually be reformulated as 'There is some way that x feels in virtue of y's having a toothache'.[19]

The colloquial phrase 'subject of experience' is thus polysemic. On the one hand it might mean the subject in whom the experience is occurring. Let me call this the 'locative of manifestation'. This host self, an inhabited self, is commonly identified with the physical human being, or the human being's brain or neuropsychological state, but Pessoa, brilliantly, gives instead a phenomenological interpretation of the notion. The phrase might also mean the subject affected by the experience. The affected subject is the one to whom the experience is addressed, so I will call this the 'accusative of manifestation'. The accusative of manifestation is, evidently, conceptually distinct from the locative of manifestation. Finally, the phrase might mean the subject who is undergoing the experience, the one who lives through the experience. This is Zahavi's 'dative of manifestation'. In labelling these disambiguations the in-S, to-S, and for-S (or by-S) positions, I am using the prepositions somewhat stipulatively, their actual use in everyday speech being rather more amorphous.

So, to return to the question with which I began this chapter, the logical form of the conscious state of mind Pessoa is in when, assuming the heteronym Caeiro, he enactively imagines himself seeing a stone, is that this conscious state, which is *in* Pessoa, is the way it feels *to* himself *for* Caeiro to see a stone. If, to appeal to my earlier terminology, Pessoa *assumes* a heteronym in simulation and *sustains* a heteronym in depersonalization, then the mental states experienced *by* this heteronym are *to* Pessoa insofar as it is assumed, and *in* Pessoa insofar as it is sustained.

These distinctions will be the foundation upon which I will seek an explanation of the concepts that are fundamental to Pessoa's philosophy. His philosophy of self consists in a set of specific, substantive, and indeed not uncontroversial, claims about the correct way to understand the in-S, to-S, and for-S positions, and the interrelationships between them. Pessoa has said that forumnal self-awareness is associated with a depersonalized sense

---

[18] Stoljar, 'The semantics of 'what it's like', p. 1172.
[19] Stoljar, 'The semantics of 'what it's like', p. 1179.

of hosting the experience and attending to it, specifically the form of attention that consists in engaging in a distinctive sort of analysis, while heteronymic self-awareness carries senses of ownership and agency with respect to the experience. When he says that 'the self who disdains his surroundings is not the same as the self who suffers or takes joy in them',[20] he is recording his discovery of the distinction between forum and heteronym. When he remarks that '…as I lucidly and intensely adapt myself to what others are feeling, I simultaneously undertake a rigorously objective analysis of their unknown self, what they think and are…',[21] what we would now say is that in 'lucidly and intensely adapting' himself Pessoa creates a new way of feeling, a new 'soul'. The claim I will make in subsequent chapters is that, for Pessoa, conscious experiences align themselves towards a particular phenomenal centre and that they resonate in a particular manner. Being at the centre of a field of experience is an accusative of manifestation, whereas an invariant manner of resonance is a dative of manifestation. I will endeavour to show that with such notions to hand we can solve the enigma of heteronymy, give precise sense to the idea of a heteronym as virtual subject, and interpret the notion of a forum qua depersonalized meeting place.

[20] *The Book of Disquiet*, #396.   [21] *The Book of Disquiet*, #305.

9

Being at the Centre

'I'm someone else in the way I'm I,' says Pessoa, meaning that in assuming a heteronym he is another I. The enigma of heteronymy is to understand how it can be, in uttering these words, that Pessoa has not said something vacuous and false. On the standard account of the way the first-person pronoun works, whenever someone utters the word 'I' it refers to whomsoever is uttering it. According to this account 'I' is a simple indexical, much like 'now' and 'here'. The reference of an indexical varies according to specific aspects of contexts of utterance, and for each indexical there is a corresponding linguistic rule, a function from contexts of utterance to referents. The rule for 'now' is that a given utterance of 'now' refers to the time of utterance, the rule of 'here' is that an utterance refers to the place of utterance—and the rule for 'I' is that an utterance refers to the person producing the utterance. So when Pessoa utters the sentence 'At the heart of my thoughts I wasn't I', what this sentence states, if 'I' is being used in conformity with the everyday rule, is that the content of his heartfelt thought is the unedifying falsehood that Pessoa is not identical to Pessoa.

We can begin to unravel the enigma if we note that a rather similar puzzle arises in the context of dreaming. As I observed above, in my discussion of Borges's story *The Circular Ruins*, I may certainly figure within my own dream, and there is therefore a conceptual distinction between the dreaming subject and the subject-within-a-dream. But is it possible for me to have a dream such that, within the dream, I am a subject other than the subject I am? This is what is required if real dreaming is to serve as a model for Pessoan heteronymic 'dreaming', the directed simulation of phenomenological landscapes in which one is an other I.

Surprisingly enough, the answer is an emphatic 'yes'. In his splendid book *Dream, Death, and The Self*, Jerome Valberg asks us to consider the following case:

Suppose I have a dream in which there are two individuals (human beings), X and JV. Yet in the dream I am not JV but X (X is me). This seems possible, but what does it mean? Not that, in the dream, JV was X.

Virtual Subjects, Fugitive Selves: Fernando Pessoa and his Philosophy. Jonardon Ganeri,
Oxford University Press (2021). © Jonardon Ganeri.
DOI: 10.1093/oso/9780198864684.001.0001

In the dream, JV and X are distinct individuals. JV is in the dream, but in the dream JV is not me. In the dream I am a human being other than the human being that I am...Given that JV and X are distinct individuals in the dream, there still exists the possibility that in the dream I am X.[1]

I believe that this passage represents the closest any contemporary philosopher has come to a rediscovery of Pessoa's insight. Notice that the sentence 'In the dream I am a human being other than the human being that I am' is a very near relative to the Pessoan thesis I earlier labelled Simulation ('I am a subject other than the subject I am'), differing only in that the context is now one of dreaming rather than simulating, and that Valberg insists on speaking only of human beings and not of subjects (I will say more about his adherence to an 'animalist' theory of selves below). The enigma of heteronymy is to understand how Simulation is not simply false, and there is an analogous puzzle here: why is it that the sentence just quoted does not simply affirm that in the dream Valberg is not Valberg? The issue is not that such a dream would then be incoherent, because dream experience might well be incoherent; the problem is that there is in this case no dreamable content at all. Just as there is nothing it is like for 2 + 2 not to equal 4, so there is simply nothing it is like for Pessoa not to be Pessoa, or for Valberg not to be Valberg.

We are to suppose I have a dream in which I and a friend are present, sitting, say, at a table in a cafe. What is peculiar about this dream, however, is that what I dream is that I am my friend, and that I am is sitting at a table with myself, JG, whom I see clearly before me. The puzzle is to know what makes it the case that, in the dream, I am X and not JG: on what grounds should we answer the question 'Which one is me?' As Valberg puts it, 'Consider the set of human beings in the cafe. One of them—this one—is the one I call 'me'. On what basis do I select him? What makes *him me*?'[2] And Valberg makes the following, extremely insightful, suggestion:

We may understand the possibility as follows. In the dream it is X, not JV, who occupied the subject position—the position occupied by JV in reality. That is, it is X, not JV, who is at the centre of the dream. In reality, JV is the one at the centre: JV is me. In the dream X occupies the position at the centre: in the dream X is me.[3]

[1] Valberg, Jerome J. *Dream, Death, and the Self.* Princeton, 2007, p. 62.
[2] Valberg, *Dream, Death, and the Self,* p. 65.
[3] Valberg, *Dream, Death, and the Self,* pp. 66–7.

Valberg's proposal is to call attention to what he calls a 'positional use' of the first person, distinct from its mundane use as an indexical, and a corresponding 'positional' conception of self. Using 'I' positionally, I am the one to whom all this is presented, the one to whom every phenomenal property is directed, or, as Valberg puts it, the one who is 'at the centre' of the manifold of presentation which he calls the experiential horizon. The manifold has a certain structure, a centre-periphery structure, and the positional conception of self is the concept of being the one located at its centre. I am the one who is at the centre, the one to whom all this is presented. 'The positional conception of self', Valberg explains,

> is the conception of a position, namely, a position within THIS, the personal horizon (my horizon)....The main idea is that it is by virtue of occupying the subject position that a particular entity, a particular human being, is 'me', the one that 'I am'. Thus the picture contains three elements: the entity that I am; the position by occupying which that entity is the one that I am; and the subject matter, my horizon, within which this position is defined.

Applying this to the case in hand, he continues,

> JV is the one at the centre of my horizon. He is the one that I am. Yet it is possible (experientially) that there be no one at the centre, or again, that it be someone other than JV. There is a sense, then, in which 'the human being that I am might not have been the human being that I am': the human being that I am, JV, might not have occupied the position at the centre of my horizon. (On this reading, we take the first occurrence of 'the human being that I am' as referential, the second as positional.) This possibility, though it may be in various ways problematic, does not contradict the necessity of identity. It is an experiential possibility, one that can be exhibited in imagination.[4]

The phenomenal field which constitutes the dream has a centre-periphery structure, there is a phenomenal position which is the centre of the field and to which its constituent phenomenal states are directed, and the use of the word 'I', in the statement 'In the dream, I am X', is to affirm that X is the one who, in the dream, occupies the centre position.

---

[4] Valberg, *Dream, Death, and the Self*, p. 264.

The reason that the possibility does not contradict the necessity of identity is that the statement 'I am X', as embedded in 'In my dream, I am X', is now revealed to be one whose logical form is not that of an identity after all, surface grammar notwithstanding. What it states is that a certain phenomenological property, the property 'being the one at the centre of this field of experience', is instantiated by X. As Valberg explains, if 'I assert 'JV is me', we may take 'is me' as replaceable by 'figures as the one at the centre of my horizon', i.e. as a predicate...To spell out the meaning of the predicate is to spell out the phenomenology of the subject position, i.e. the positional conception of the self'.[5] Again, 'Assuming the positional use of the first person, the meaning of 'JV is me (the one that I am)' is: JV figures as the one at the centre of my horizon. The 'is' in the expression 'is me', then, is not the 'is' of identity, nor is 'me' a singular term; rather the whole expression 'is me' functions as a predicate'.[6] When used positionally, in other words, an utterance of 'I' is equivalent to a descriptive demonstrative, namely, 'The one who is at the centre of this field of experience'.

The positional conception of self is one which Pessoa quite explicitly puts at the heart of his philosophy. He describes it with insight and sensitivity:

> I've never succeeded in seeing myself from the outside. No mirror can show us ourself from outside, because no mirror can take us out of ourself. We would need a different soul, a different way of looking and thinking. If I were an actor projected on a screen, or if I recorded my voice on records, I'm certain that I still wouldn't know what I am on the outside, because, like it or not, and no matter what I might record of myself, I'm always here inside, enclosed by high walls, on the private estate of my consciousness of me.[7]

The indexical and positional conceptions are clearly distinguished here, the indexical use featuring in 'if I recorded my voice' and the positional use in 'I'm always here inside'. In an even clearer reference to the positional conception, he writes,

> There remains something obscure
> In the centre of my being...[8]

---

[5] Valberg, *Dream, Death, and the Self*, p. 334.
[6] Valberg, *Dream, Death, and the Self*, p. 336.   [7] *The Book of Disquiet*, #338.
[8] [Qualquer coisa de obscuro permanece / No centro do meu ser....] Sabino, Maria do Rosário Marques, and Sereno, Adelaide Maria Monteiro, eds., *Novas Poesias Inéditas. Obras completas de Fernando Pessoa*, no. 10. Lisbon: Ática, 1973, p. 92. Arquivo Pessoa, text 2458.

The phrase 'my being' is phenomenological, one's phenomenal being has a centre, and there is something, something obscure, at its centre. Elsewhere Pessoa appeals directly to the idea of a phenomenological centre, several times exploiting the metaphor of a well and its walls to describe the structure of the field of experience:

> My soul is a black whirlpool, a vast vertigo circling a void, the racing of an infinite ocean around a hole in nothing. And in these waters which are more a churning than actual waters float the images of all I've seen and heard in the world—houses, faces, books, boxes, snatches of music and syllables of voices all moving in a sinister and bottomless swirl. And amid all this confusion I, what's truly I, am the centre that exists only in the geometry of the abyss: I'm the nothing around which everything spins, existing only so that it can spin, being a centre only because every circle has one. I, what's truly I, am a well without walls but with the wall's viscosity, the centre of everything with nothing around it.[9]

Again, 'We are two abysses—a well staring at the sky.' [10] 'I feel like a mere void, the illusion of a soul, the locus of a being, a conscious darkness where a strange insect vainly seeks at least the warm memory of a light.'[11] And, to repeat a quotation already discussed, 'I am nothing—just an abstract centre of impersonal sensations.'[12] So the sensorium's structure, the structure of the 'all this' in 'perhaps all this is a dream', is elegantly likened by Pessoa to a well, without definite boundaries but nevertheless in some way bounded, and when he declares that 'I, what's truly I, am a well without walls but with the wall's viscosity', he is exactly describing the positional conception of self and the positional use of the first person. As the centre of a well is that to which the surfaces of the well face, so the sensations that constitute the phenomenal field face towards a phenomenal centre, and the positional use of 'I' is to describe oneself as the one who is at this centre: 'I'm the one here in myself, it's me.'[13]

We can now account for the experiential possibility of a dream in which I am not myself by saying that in such a case the self-within-the-dream is conceived of positionally: the one at the centre of this field of experience, the one to whom the experience is addressed, is not Valberg but his friend, X. It is to his friend that the phenomenal items which constitute the dream present. In

---

[9] *The Book of Disquiet*, #262.   [10] *The Book of Disquiet*, #11.
[11] *The Book of Disquiet*, #219.   [12] *The Book of Disquiet*, #208.
[13] *A Little Larger*, p. 240.

an appropriation of Valberg's example, the philosopher Mark Johnston has Sally report that in her dream her father asked her to marry him, adding, 'But the funny thing is, in that dream I *was* my father.'[14] He says,

> I can understand Sally's claim that in her dream she was her father. She means something like this: the human being who occupied the central phenomenological position in her dream, the one to whom events in the dream were presented, the one who apparently initiated action from this centre, was her father, Mr. Smith. Sally was just another human being appearing in the dream. Sally was not occupying the position at the phenomenological centre of her dream. Sally was the dreamer of her dream, not doubt about that. But this is compatible with the central phenomenological position in her dream being occupied by another human being, or by a rational parrot, or by an angel. And so it is compatible with the human being, Sally Smith, turning up in the dream and addressing the person at the centre of her dream. And so it is compatible with Sally being proposed to by the one who is at the centre of her dream—as it turns out, by her father.[15]

Johnston agrees with Valberg, and with Pessoa, when he says that 'it is a contingent claim, and one that is not always true, that in my dreams I am the human being Johnston'.[16]

With the positional conception of self to hand, a solution to the enigma of heteronymy is available. What, then, of the fundamental Pessoan distinction between heteronymic and forumnal self-awareness? In the next chapter I will demonstrate that an interpretation of the notion of a forum, a meeting place or harbour for heteronymic subjectivity, can also be derived from the positional conception of self. What I will be at pains to stress is that the forum is not a distinct self standing behind the heteronyms. In fact it represents a rather more interesting development in the theory of subjectivity. The shifting, unfixed, contingent inhabitation of the subject position is phenomenologically linked with a sense of oneself as estranged, as a fugitive, and it is this sense of oneself as phenomenologically fugitive which is the basis of Pessoan depersonalization.

---

[14] Johnston, Mark. *Surviving Death*. Princeton, 2010, p. 150.
[15] Johnston, *Surviving Death*, p. 150.   [16] Johnston, *Surviving Death*, p. 150.

10

The Fugitive and the Forum

I, the one that is me, am the one who is at the centre of all this. In his discussions of the multiplicity of I, Pessoa has shown, though, that this state is not a stable one, that the one that I am is not static and single but, with each new heteronym assumed, another I becomes me. I want now to consider how this fact manifests itself within self-awareness. Pessoa describes the phenomenology in one of his most famous, and most autobiographical, poems—the poem he calls his 'Autopsychography':

> I'm a fugitive.
> I was shut up in myself
> As soon as I was born.
> But I managed to flee.
> If people get tired
> Of being in the same place,
> Why shouldn't they tire
> Of having the same self?
> My soul seeks me out,
> But I keep on the run
> And sincerely hope
> I'll never be found.
> Oneness is a prison.
> To be myself is to not be.
> I'll live as a fugitive
> But live really and truly.[1]

A fugitive is someone on the run, someone not at home, someone whose life is transient and ephemeral. Pessoa is on the run from himself, meaning from the one who has, since childhood, hogged the subject position. The way to live truly is to embrace the contingency in that position's inhabitation.

[1] *A Little Larger*, p. 315.

Virtual Subjects, Fugitive Selves: Fernando Pessoa and his Philosophy. Jonardon Ganeri, Oxford University Press (2021). © Jonardon Ganeri.
DOI: 10.1093/oso/9780198864684.001.0001

Pessoa also describes the feeling as one of estrangement, for one can't feel completely at home in oneself when one is alert to the ever-present possibility of a shift in the occupation of the subject position:

No one imagined that at my side there was always another, who was in fact I. They always supposed I was identical to myself. Their houses sheltered me, their hands shook mine, and they saw me walk down the street as if I were there; but the I that I am was never in their living rooms, the I whose life I live has no hands for others to shake, and the I that I know walks down no streets, unless the streets are all streets, nor is seen in them by others, unless he himself is all the others. We all live far away and anonymous; disguised, we suffer as unknowns. For some, however, this distance between oneself and one's self is never revealed; for others it is occasionally enlightened, to their horror or grief, by a flash without limits; but for still others this is the painful daily reality of life.[2]

In this passage the 'distance between oneself and one's self' refers, I suggest, to the sense of estrangement intrinsic to a fugitive phenomenology. I, the one that I am, am forever on the move.

It is the fugitive who here refers to itself as 'the I that I am', and who says, in the first person, 'For me it's never I who thinks, speaks or acts. It's always one of my dreams, which I momentarily embody, that thinks, speaks and acts for me. I open my mouth, but it's I-another who speaks. The only thing I feel to be really mine is a huge incapacity, a vast emptiness, an incompetence for everything that is life.'[3] We can understand better now what Pessoa means when he says that 'There remains something obscure / In the centre of my being....'[4] What he refers to here as an obscurity in the positional conception is nothing but the fact that the centre is never more than contingently occupied by any one of the multitude of I's that I am. The fugitive in self-awareness is just another name for the awareness of this contingency, the unsettling knowledge that whomsoever is the one at the centre, he or she is only contingently and temporarily me.

Let me call this the fugitive use of 'I', and the fugitive conception of self. The fugitive is the one who, in sustaining a multiplicity of heteronymic identities, feels nothing but estrangement, an emptiness of personality. Estrangement here consists not in *disidentification* with any of the

[2] *The Book of Disquiet*, #433.   [3] *The Book of Disquiet*, #215.
[4] *Nova Poesias Inéditas*, p. 92.

heteronyms but rather in the merely *contingent identification* with each and every one. 'My God, my God, who am I watching? How many am I? What is this gap between me and myself?' Pessoa, as Soares, asks.[5] And, again, 'By thinking so much, I became echo and abyss. By delving within, I made myself into many.'[6] It is clear, indeed, that the 'I' of the *Book of Disquiet* is the 'I' of the fugitive:

> Not even I know if this I that I'm disclosing to you, in these meandering pages, actually exists or is but a fictitious, aesthetic concept I've made of myself. Yes, that's right. I live aesthetically as someone else. I've sculpted my life like a statue of matter that's foreign to my being. Having employed my self-awareness in such a purely artistic way, and having become so completely external to myself, I sometimes no longer recognize myself.[7]

'I'm a nomad in my self-awareness,'[8] Pessoa says, with scientific precision. This is the most exact imaginable definition of the fugitive conception of self. The heteronyms are indeed, in Zbigniew Kotowicz's elegant phrase, the many voices of a nomadic soul.[9]

We have now a way to make better sense of the role of the notion of depersonalization in Pessoa's philosophy of self, and thus of the forum and of forumnal self-awareness. Pessoan depersonalization is a keen self-awareness that the occupier of the centre at any moment, 'the one that I am', is there only contingently. José Saramago, in his novel *The Year of the Death of Ricardo Reis*, captures the flavour of the idea very well when he has Reis say, '...or do I think what I'm thinking in the thinking-place that is me...Who is using me in order to feel and think, and among those innumerable people who live within me, which am I, who, quem, Quain, what thoughts and feelings might there be that I don't share...?'[10] Indeed, as Mark Sabine keenly observes, the Reis of Saramago's novel 'characterizes the self as a hermetic forum for thought and sensation...'.[11] This is the depersonalized use of 'I,' the use that is grounded in impartial introspective attention, when one's

---

[5] *The Book of Disquiet*, #213.   [6] *The Book of Disquiet*, #93.
[7] *The Book of Disquiet*, #114.   [8] *The Book of Disquiet*, #107.
[9] Kotowicz, Zbigniew. *Fernando Pessoa: Voices of a Nomadic Soul.* Shearsman Press, 2008.
[10] Saramago, José. *The Year of the Death of Ricardo Reis*, translated by Giovanni Ponteiro. Harvill Press, 1988, p. 24.
[11] Sabine, Mark. 'Saramago's 'other' Pessoas and 'Pessoan' others: Heteronymic creation and the ethics of alterity'. In *Pessoa in an Intertextual Web: Influence and Innovation*, edited by David Frier. Legenda, 2012, pp. 148–71, at p.154.

experience is registered, first-personally, not as lived through but as observed.

Pessoa is not alone in seeking to call attention to the phenomenology of the fugitive self. Jorge Luis Borges provides a fine depiction of fugitive phenomenology in his story *Everything and Nothing*. He presents Shakespeare as becoming many in order to disguise an inner emptiness:

> Thus while his body, in whorehouses and taverns around London, lived its life as body, the soul that lived inside it would be Caesar, who ignores the admonition of the sibyl, and Juliet, who hates the lark, and Macbeth, who speaks on the moor with the witches who are also the Fates, the Three Weird Sisters. No one was as many men as that man—that man whose repertoire, like that of the Egyptian Proteus, was all the appearances of being. From time to time he would leave a confession in one corner or another of the work, certain that it would not be deciphered; Richard says that inside himself, he plays the part of many, and Iago says, with curious words, *I am not what I am.* . . . History adds that before or after he died, he discovered himself standing before God, and said to Him: I, who have been so many men in vain, wish to be one, to be myself. God's voice answered him out of a whirlwind: *I, too, am not I.* I dreamed the world as you, Shakespeare, dreamed your own work, and among the forms of my dreams are you, who like me are many, yet no one.[12]

Borges portrays Shakespeare, we are now able to say, as heteronymically simulating each of his protagonists, as becoming them. In so doing, the fugitive is brought into view, a 'nobody' who is on the run from his 'nobodiness', the nobodiness of a self which can truly affirm 'I am not I'.[13] I think of myself as only contingently associated with any of the subjects that I have lived as, and in so doing conceive of myself as a nobody who has been many.[14]

---

[12] Borges, Jorge Luis. *Everything and Nothing*. In his *Collected Fictions*, translated by Andrew Hurley. Penguin, 1999, p. 319. Another of his stories, *Borges and I* (*Collected Fictions*, p. 324), can be read as describing a similar contingency.

[13] *Othello* I.i.66. For Iago, perhaps, the intention was only that appearance and reality had come apart. In Borges's hands, that is certainly a deliberate inversion of the phrase in *Exodus* 3:14 by which Jehovah defines himself to Moses: 'I am that I am.' There is also, perhaps, a hint of the concept of the fugitive in *Sāṃkhya-kārikā* 64: 'I do not exist, nothing is mine, I am not.'

[14] I will say more about the suggestion, in *Everything and Nothing*, that we are all, as it were, the heteronyms of God in the final chapter, 'The Cosmos and I'.

The fugitive, therefore, is not a self *distinct from* the multiple heteronymic selves. That is the point Pessoa makes when he writes, 'I look at them. Not a single one am I, being all.'[15] Here, the I that looks at its heteronyms is not a self distinct from them because, precisely, any given moment it is one or more of them. It is just that thinking of oneself positionally entails an estrangement in the phenomenology of one's self-awareness. This is surely the import of the first stanza in Pessoa's celebrated poem, which sees a direct relationship between the multiplicity of I and the phenomenology of the fugitive:

> I don't know how many souls I have.
> I've changed at every moment.
> I always feel like a stranger.
> I've never seen or found myself.[16]

In my inability to identify with any one of my many heteronyms to the exclusion of all others, I find myself estranged from them all. The phenomenology of the fugitive is that of introspective attention, an impartial analysis of the multiplicity of the inner lives which are one's own. The subject position as such, whichever heteronym is assumed, is then rightly conceptualized as a meeting place, a forum, for them all. So it is the positional use of 'I' which underwrites and explains its forumnal use. The fugitive is thus the locative of manifestation, which is, therefore, not the human body or some part of it but an aspect of phenomenality. There is no fugitive self in Orhan Pamuk's *My Name is Red*, but only a sequence of fields of experience, the occupants of whose centres referring to themselves in turn as 'I'. The character who speaks in the first person in one chapter is in no position truly to affirm, 'In the next chapter I will be so-and-so.' The fugitive self is also what is absent in the phenomenology of the sufferer of MPD or any other 'confederation' of selves: an alter who is currently 'out' cannot truly affirm, 'Ten minutes ago I was so-and-so,' referring to the alter who was 'out' then. Elsewhere, in his essay 'On the Porlock Man,' Pessoa speaks of 'the stranger which is us', an internalized version of the visitor who interrupted Coleridge in the midst of his composition of *Kubla Khan*, and which is for Pessoa someone who 'being us, is not "somebody", [and so] is a nobody'.

[15] *Fernando Pessoa & Co.: Selected Poems*, p. 118.
[16] *Fernando Pessoa & Co.: Selected Poems*, p. 243.

The Porlock man, this powerful metaphor for an essential aspect of poetic creation, is reconceptualized by Pessoa as the fugitive self.[17]

I have drawn on the idea that there is a positional conception of self, and a positional use of the first person over and above its mundane indexical use, to present a solution to the enigma of heteronymy and to give an account of the type of self-awareness in play when one thinks of oneself in forumnal self-awareness as a depersonalized meeting place, a harbour for the heteronyms, the locative of manifestation. It is time now to reflect on the nature of the occupants of the subject position, and so to return to the analysis of heteronymy and heteronymic self-awareness. Heteronymic self-hood is, as I hinted at before and now want to demonstrate in greater detail, a matter of for-me-ness, the dative of manifestation. The aspect of phenomenality this concerns is *how* an experience is for me, what it is to *live through* that experience. My argument will be that Pessoa's 'styles' or 'manners' of feeling are adverbial aspects of the phenomenology of a field of experience, as distinct from those structural aspects to which the positional conception applies. A heteronym, a virtual self, tracks a subject-invariant way of feeling, a notion that is underwritten and explained by a *non-positional* conception of self.

---

[17] 'O homen de Porlock'. *Fradique* 1 (Feb. 15, 1934), pp. 7–9, at p. 8. See Miranda, Rui Gonçalves. *Personal Infinitive: Inflecting Fernando Pessoa.* Critical, Cultural & Communications Press, 2017, pp. 182–99; Castro, Mariana Gray de. 'Pessoa, Coleridge, homens de Porlock e dias triunfais'. *Revista Estranhar Pessoa* 1 (2014), pp. 58–70.

11

Landscapes of Presence

Looking about me, I think that perhaps all *this* is a dream. How is the referent of 'this' to be understood? Valberg describes it as 'the subject matter', a subject matter in which someone 'figures' as being the one at the centre, and he uses the term 'horizonal' to describe its overall shape. A horizon is the limit of the visible, a virtual boundary dependent on the location of the perceiver. So we can speak of 'my horizon', and Valberg is quick to note that the use of the first person in this phrase cannot be reduced to either the positional or the barely indexical uses: 'Clearly, the "my" in "my horizon" is not yet another positional use of the first person, as if by "the horizon that is mine" we might mean: the horizon that is at the centre of my horizon.'[1] Again, 'Within the expression "my horizon", the expression "my" does not function referentially. Unlike the "my" in (say) "my car", the possessive "my", it does not refer to an owner. It simply expresses aloneness, and thus, despite the grammatical analogy with the possessive "my", it does not refer at all.'[2] Thus, and this was Wittgenstein's famous point about solipsism, I would be better off speaking simply of *the* horizon.

There are two, rather different, ideas here. One is that there is a non-positional, 'horizonal', use of the first person, a use that is in play when I say that I am the one at the centre of *my* field of experience. There is evidence of this thought in Pessoa, who elegantly refers to the shape of the phenomenal field as the 'geometry of the abyss', where the abyss is likened to a well, a well 'without walls but with the wall's viscosity':

> And amid all this confusion I, what's truly I, am the centre that exists only in the geometry of the abyss: I'm the nothing around which everything spins, existing only so that it can spin, being a centre only because every

[1] Valberg, J. J. *Dream, Death, and the Self.* Princeton, 2007, p. 337.
[2] Valberg, *Dream, Death, and the Self*, p. 338.

Virtual Subjects, Fugitive Selves: Fernando Pessoa and his Philosophy. Jonardon Ganeri,
Oxford University Press (2021). © Jonardon Ganeri.
DOI: 10.1093/oso/9780198864684.001.0001

circle has one. I, what's truly I, am a well without walls but with the wall's viscosity, the centre of everything with nothing around it.[3]

The field has a fluid but firm boundary, a limit which is its horizon.

The second idea, though, is that the 'my' in 'my horizon' expresses merely aloneness, that there is an ineluctable solipsism in the way each of us finds ourselves. Valberg's claim is that the 'my' in 'my personal horizon' merely stands in for the definite description[4] because 'my' horizon claims to include every other:

> It is, we might say, part of what it is to be at the centre of a horizon that the one at the centre, the one for whom it is 'mine', views the horizon as the all-inclusive horizon. So this must hold for every subject, for anyone at the centre...But I know that it is like that from within all horizons. I know, then that my horizon is just one among many, coordinate with all other horizons. The thing to see is that the claim my horizon makes to preeminence enters into its metaphysical status as one among many.[5]

Pessoa, again, anticipates the point: 'One of my constant preoccupations is to understand how other people can exist, how there can be souls that aren't mine, consciousnesses that have nothing to do with my own, which—because it's a consciousness—seems to me like the only one.'[6] *My* field of consciousness is the field in which everything is presented, and so it presents itself to me as the all-inclusive field and seems to me as if the only one. 'The universe isn't mine: it's me,'[7] Pessoa has Soares say, in an uncanny echo of Wittgenstein's succinct comment, 'I am my world.'[8] And Pessoa agrees too that whatever it is that the 'my' in 'my horizon' signifies, it is not a relation of possession: 'Do we possess the soul? Listen carefully: no, we don't. Not even our own soul is ours...We don't even possess our own sensation...We do not possess our sensations, and through them we cannot possess ourselves.'[9]

Johnston objects to the solipsism implicit in Valberg's notion of the horizon, which, he thinks, is due to the fact that the horizon is 'a highly theorised object, one that only comes into view by way of an elegant philosophical

---

[3] *The Book of Disquiet*, #262.   [4] Valberg, *Dream, Death, and the Self*, p. 338.
[5] Valberg, *Dream, Death, and the Self*, pp. 130–1.   [6] *The Book of Disquiet*, #317.
[7] *The Book of Disquiet*, #123.
[8] Wittgenstein, Ludwig. *Tractatus Logico-Philosophicus*, translated by C. K. Ogden (Routledge, 1922), 5.63.
[9] *The Book of Disquiet*, #363.

interpretation of what threatens to cease to be with one's death.[10] Seeking to domesticate the idea, he prefers a revised characterization of the phenomenal field: he describes it as 'this arena of presence and action'. The idea of an arena is that of 'a mental quasi-space', an 'all-inclusive psychological field',[11] 'an inclusive mental field',[12] a field comprising 'the visual, auditory and other sensory fields, the bodily field, and the field of thought and of action experienced from the inside as willed',[13] all of which are 'organised around a phenomenological centre, a sort of virtual limit where perspectival modes of presentation converge.'[14] The psychological fields constitute an arena of presence which is 'organized around an implied centre that is a merely intentional object' and whose virtual boundaries are such that 'there is no answer to the question of what is on the other side'.[15] The demonstrative description 'the centre of *this* arena of presence and action' is allocentric, that is, a description anybody can make from their own point of view: 'There is one such arena *here*, and I assume you can truly make a corresponding remark about your own case.'[16] The phenomenology of mine-ness, Johnston suggests, is not that of a solipsistic 'aloneness' but simply a sense of the wholeness and unity that a centred arena exhibits. He says, 'The felt 'mine-ness' of my mental acts is not itself the awareness of a common intrinsic constituent of those acts, as it were, the mental self or ego at the subject pole. It is a feeling of fit; a sense that these present mental acts cohere with a dominant stream of mental life.'[17] In the case of a Cotard's patient, on the other hand, 'there is no longer the kind of experiential fit that makes for the sensed "mine-ness" of experience. The arena and its centre are not in view.'[18] Johnston, however, does not say more about what, precisely, a 'feeling of fit' is meant to be, and the obvious objection to such an account is that I can be aware of disharmonies in the arena of presence that is mine.

As we might expect from a world-class poet who is also an analytical student of his own first-personal phenomenology, Pessoa provides a rich set of descriptions of the all-inclusive psychological field and its structure. The metaphor that seems to recur most frequently is that of a landscape: 'Eternal tourists of ourselves, there is no landscape but what we are.'[19] 'The geography of our consciousness of reality is an endless complexity of irregular coasts,

[10] Johnston, Mark. *Surviving Death*. Princeton, 2010, p. 186.
[11] Johnston, *Surviving Death*, p. 182.   [12] Johnston, *Surviving Death*, p. 224.
[13] Johnston, *Surviving Death*, p. 224.   [14] Johnston, *Surviving Death*, p. 182.
[15] Johnston, *Surviving Death*, p. 224–5.   [16] Johnston, *Surviving Death*, p. 140.
[17] Johnston, *Surviving Death*, p. 167.   [18] Johnston, *Surviving Death*, p. 167.
[19] *The Book of Disquiet*, #123.

low and high mountains, and myriad lakes.'[20] 'To dream is to find ourselves. You're going to be the Columbus of your soul. You're going to set out to discover your own landscapes.'[21] 'The true landscapes are those that we ourselves create since, being their gods, we see them as they truly are, which is however we created them.'[22] 'All these half-tones of the soul's consciousness create in us a painful landscape, an eternal sunset of what we are. The sensation we come to have of ourselves is of a deserted field at dusk, sad with reeds next to a river without boats, its glistening waters blackening between wide banks.'[23] The psychological field is also described as 'a forest of estrangement',[24] and again as 'a city in the Orient'.[25] It is my 'private estate': 'I'm always here inside, enclosed by high walls, on the private estate of my consciousness of me.'[26] Pessoa's English poem 'A temple', from 1907, might be read as an allegorical description of the structure of the psychological field:

> I have built my temple—wall and face—
> Outside the idea of space,
> Complex-built as a full-rigged ship;
> I made its walls of my fears,
> Its turrets made of weird thoughts and tears—
> And that strange temple, thus unfurled
> Like a death's-head flag, that like a whip
> Stinging around my soul is curled,
> Is far more real than the world.[27]

The experiential field is neither merely a horizon nor just an arena but a temple in the form of a whip curled around its centre, my soul. Two distinct uses of the first person are on display here. While the 'my' in 'my soul' is used positionally, referring to whomsoever is at the centre, the 'my' in 'my temple' is the horizonal use: the field of awareness and consciousness that is my personal field of awareness and consciousness. 'I am my own landscape,' writes Pessoa, again invoking the two distinct uses.[28]

---

[20] *The Book of Disquiet*, #338.
[21] 'The art of effective dreaming (I)', *The Book of Disquiet*, p. 400.
[22] *The Book of Disquiet*, #138.   [23] *The Book of Disquiet*, #196.
[24] 'If I take one of my sensations and unravel it so as to use it to weave the inner reality I call "The Forest of Estrangement"…'. 'Sentimental education', *The Book of Disquiet*, p. 456.
[25] 'My imagination is a city in the Orient'. 'Imperial legend', *The Book of Disquiet*, p.416.
[26] *The Book of Disquiet*, #338.   [27] *A Little Larger*, p. 410.
[28] *Fernando Pessoa & Co.: Selected Poems*, p. 243.

We have already introduced the idea that experience embeds an implicit 'for-me' grammatical place, that is to say that there is a dative of manifestation, a way in which experience presents itself as for-me. Evidently this is what makes a landscape of experience mine in the relevant sense. What, though, actually is for-me-ness, the subjective character of experience, the subjective dimension? Marie Guillot states that 'everyone agrees that subjective character has to do with the fact that the existence of an experience *resonates in a particular way* with the subject in whom it occurs.'[29] Dan Zahavi, in the latest formulation of a position which he now calls Experiential Minimalism, defends a reflexivist construal of the concept. On a reflexive interpretation, what makes an experience for a subject is that it, the experience, is aware of itself:

> A guiding idea has been that if we wish to do justice to the subjective character of experiential episodes, we should acknowledge that episodes characterized by a subjective what-it-is-likeness are not merely episodes that happen to take place in a subject, regardless of whether the subject is aware of them or not. Rather, the what-it-is-likeness of phenomenal states is properly speaking a what-it-is-like-for-me-ness. On this view, experiential processes are intrinsically conscious and hence self-revealing. They are characterized by an inherent reflexive (not reflective) or pre-reflective self-consciousness in the weak sense that they are like something for the subject, i.e. in virtue of their mere existence, they are phenomenally manifest to the subject of those experiences.[30]

Zahavi here begins with our familiar observation about the grammatical form of that what-it-is-like construction, that there is a covert subject position generated by the infinitive, and then goes on to propose that for-me-ness is equivalent to reflexive self-awareness. Another prominent exponent of the view, Uriah Kriegel, likewise affirms that 'a mental state has subjective character just in case it is for the subject, in the sense that the subject has a certain awareness of it'.[31]

---

[29] Guillot, Marie. 'I me mine: on a confusion concerning the subjective character of experience'. *Review of Philosophy and Psychology* 8 (2017), pp. 23–53, at p. 31.

[30] Zahavi, Dan. 'Consciousness and selfhood: Getting clearer on for-me-ness and mineness'. In *The Oxford Handbook of the Philosophy of Consciousness*, edited by Uriah Kriegel. Oxford, 2020, chapter 29.

[31] Kriegel, Uriah. *Subjective Consciousness: A Self-Representational Theory*. Oxford, 2009, p. 38.

The idea that for-me-ness consists in phenomenal self-disclosure is certainly an important and powerful one, prominently defended in the twentieth century by Jean-Paul Sartre, Dieter Henrich and Manfred Frank; and by Dignāga, Dharmakīrti, and other thinkers in Indian andTibetan Buddhist traditions.[32] Yet from a Pessoan perspective it is inconsistent with a fundamental datum about conscious experience, the discovery of heteronymic subjectivity. If for-me-ness consists in reflexive self-representation, then no distinction can be made between the for-me-ness associated with Caeiro and the for-me-ness associated with Reis. The trouble with reflexivist theories of subjectivity is that they are attenuated, in the sense that they do not permit a phenomenological distinction to be drawn between one subject and another. It would be as if the members of a group of people each affirms that their own country is the best, and we are expected to read off their actual nationalities from these bare reflexive affirmations. For-me-ness is indeed 'the categorical basis of our capacity for first-person thought',[33] but just for that reason it cannot consist in mere reflexive self-representation. We need more than reflexivity: what we need is that idea that there are distinct invariant ways of feeling indexing distinct subjects. Insofar, indeed, as heteronymic subjectivity in this way presents a challenge and a rival to other accounts of the very nature of subjectivity, I would venture that Pessoa's analytical phenomenology should be recognized as a distinct strand in the phenomenological tradition, and a very original one.

Preferable for our present purposes is the more generic formulation proposed by Guillot, that what it means to say that an experiential episode is for-a-subject is that the experience *resonates in a particular way* with the subject in whom it occurs. If the qualificative character of the experience is the way the experience feels to the subject, and so varies from one experiential episode to the next, the subjective character of an experience is comparatively invariant across the experiential life of a subject, but varies from one subject to another. So the 'two dimensions' of phenomenality are two dimensions of variation in the way an experience feels, and we can say that the heteronym Caeiro is a particular, Caeiroish, way for experience to feel. That is just Pessoa's claim discussed earlier:

---

[32] See Zahavi, Dan. 'Reflexivity, transparency and illusionism'. *Protosociology* 36 (2020), pp. 142–56; my 'Self-intimation, memory and personal identity'. *Journal of Indian Philosophy* 27 (1999), pp. 469–83.

[33] Zahavi, Dan, and Kriegel, Uriah. 'For-me-ness: What it is and what it is not'. In Dahlstrom, Daniel O., Elpidorou, Andreas, and Hopp, Walter, eds., *Philosophy of Mind and Phenomenology: Conceptual and Empirical Approaches*. London: Routledge, 2015, p. 49.

The only way you can have new sensations is by forging a new soul. It's useless to try to feel new things without feeling them in a new way, and you can't feel in a new way without changing your soul. For things are what we feel they are—how long have you known this without yet knowing it?—and the only way for there to be new things, for us to feel new things, is for there to be some novelty in how we feel them.[34]

A Pessoan 'way of feeling' is a subject-specific adverbial feature of a landscape of sensation. Pessoa does not say much more than that, but once again we can appeal to contemporary theory to substantiate the idea.

To give the idea greater precision, let me introduce the idea of a 'mode of consciousness', as recently defended by Timothy Bayne and Jakob Hohwy.[35] They describe modes of consciousness as 'global ways of being conscious',[36] 'global' in that they 'characterize the overall conscious state of a creature',[37] and they give as examples the waking state, the hypnotic state, stupor, rapid eye movement, deep sleep, and so on. There are, they go on to suggest, three dimensions in the modality of consciousness—the dimensions, respectively, of content, structure, and function. The content dimension incorporates such ideas as that modes involve restrictions or limits on the number of items and the types of content that are available to a subject. The structure dimension appeals to the idea that a field of consciousness is structured by attention into thematic focal point, along with marginal and peripheral regions. The modality of consciousness expresses itself both in how attention structures the field of awareness and how it is controlled.[38] Finally, the functional dimension has to do with the role of consuming systems, systems that employ conscious states in the service of a cognitive or behavioural task.

My proposal is to analyse a Pessoan 'way of feeling' as a *subject-invariant* mode of consciousness, a mode of consciousness that is comparatively invariant within and across the experiential life of a given subject, but which varies from one subject to the next. Along a content dimension, this would imply that there are subject-specific limits or restrictions on the quantity and type of content available to consciousness. One might speculate, for

---

[34] *The Book of Disquiet*, #301.

[35] Bayne, Timothy, and Hohwy, Jakob. 'Modes of consciousness'. In Walter Sinnott-Armstrong, ed. *Finding Consciousness: The Neuroscience, Ethics, and Law of Severe Brain Damage*. Oxford, 2016, pp. 57–80.

[36] Bayne and Hohwy, 'Modes of consciousness', p. 57.

[37] Bayne and Hohwy, 'Modes of consciousness', p. 59.

[38] Watzl, Sebastian. *Structuring Mind: The Nature of Attention and How it Shapes Consciousness*. Oxford, 2017, ch. 9.

example, that part of what is unique to Alberto Caeiro's way of feeling is that the only content available to him is nonconceptual. Along the structural dimension, suppose one believes that fields of awareness have structures which exemplify phenomenal features that are irreducible to the component phenomenal properties that constitute them (that there is something it is like to experience the given structure a landscape of sensation has). If one can also isolate aspects of phenomenal structure which are relatively invariant across the experiential life of a person, then one can identify the phenomenal features of such invariant structural aspects with a Pessoan 'way of feeling'. The mode of consciousness of Ricardo Reis is subject to a structural constraint, his experience conforming with a classical ideal of rule and order.

With respect to the functional dimension, one would, again, seek to isolate ways in which consuming systems are employed that are specific to particular subjects and invariant across their experiential lives. Take Álvaro de Campos: is it not the case that insofar as his way of feeling consists in a bracketing of the 'as they are' in 'feel things as they are', the consumer system responsible for reality-checking is uniquely unengaged? I do not think that Pessoa himself had any specific account of 'ways of feeling' in mind, and it is an open question, one that is to be answered as much by drawing on empirical work in cognitive psychology as on philosophical analysis, as to which formulation of the notion will be the best one to adopt. For our current purposes it is enough to note that if one grants that the idea of a mode of consciousness is a scientifically respectable one, then a 'way of feeling' or 'style of feeling' or 'manner of resonance' is easy enough to analyse as a subject-invariant mode of consciousness. Introducing a heteronym simply provides the subject with respect to whom such a mode of consciousness is invariant a name. And, I have suggested, Pessoa's three principal heteronyms are exemplary of the three modalities of content, structure, and function.

Pessoa does say a little more about ways of feeling in a famous passage in which he imagines being a fly:

When I laid my hands on the desk and looked at what was there with a gaze that must have been heavy with dead worlds, the first thing I saw, with my physical eyes, was a blowfly (that soft buzzing that didn't belong to the office!) poised on top of the inkstand. I looked at it from the depths of the abyss, anonymous and attentive. It was coloured by green shades of black-blue, and its shiny repulsiveness wasn't ugly. A life! Who knows for what supreme forces—gods or demons of Truth in whose shadow we roam—I may be nothing but a shiny fly that alights in front of them for a moment or two? A facile hypothesis? Maybe. But I didn't think: I felt. It was carnally, directly, with profound and dark horror that I made this ludicrous comparison. I was a fly when I compared myself to one. I really felt like a fly when I imagined I felt like one. And I felt I had a flyish soul, slept flyishly and was flyishly withdrawn. And what's more horrifying is that I felt, at the same time, like myself. I automatically raised my eyes towards the ceiling, lest a lofty wooden ruler should swoop down to swat me, as I might swat that fly.[39]

Thomas Nagel's famous scepticism about knowing what it is like to be a bat is not shared by Pessoa, who found little difficulty enactively imagining that he is a fly. As Pessoa makes clear, when he imagined that he is a fly, it is not merely the case that he imagined that there is a fly at the experiential landscape's centre but that he had a 'flyish soul' and felt 'flyishly': the psychological field is filled with 'flyish' experiential properties, sensations that resonate in a flyish manner. So we should reparse the question 'What is it like to be a fly?' as 'How is it to me [conceived positionally, the one at the centre] for me [as a fly] to feel?' In saying that it is a fly which 'figures' as the one at the centre of a landscape of sensation, what is meant is that the for-me-ness of the sensations, their manner of resonance, is flyish. If it is a fly which figures as the one at the centre, then the subject matter—its contents, the way it is organized, its manner of presentation—is specific to the fly. If, in imagination or in a dream, I am a fly, this does not mean that a fly just happens to occupy the centre position in a field of experience that is qualitatively identical to that of the human being I am. It means that the mode—in structure, content, and function—is that of a fly, is flyish.

Heteronymic self-awareness, then, is manner of resonance or style of feeling, and that is just what the for-me-ness, the subjective dimension, consists in. It is the 'my' in 'my landscape of sensation;' it is, therefore, the horizonal conception of self. Maintaining an interdependence between the heteronymic and the horizonal conceptions of self preserves the important insight that there is a non-positional use of 'I', but without the solipsism intrinsic to Valberg's overtheorized conception of the horizon or the excessive strictness in Johnston's notion of fit.

[39] *The Book of Disquiet*, #334.

12

Virtual Subjects

The positional conception is the conception of oneself as the one at the centre of a landscape of presence. The positional conception is essential to a solution to the enigma of heteronymy, and so to a sound interpretation of Pessoa's philosophy. Our task now is to talk about the types of entity which occupy this centre position. What occupies that position? Given that it is evidently a self or subject which does so, the task is to say more about the nature of selves.

One possibility is that the occupants of the subject position are Cartesian souls, purely mental substances. Although Pessoa is happy to use the word 'soul' (*alma*), it is clear from his description of 'amming' himself as a process of self-creation that he has wholly broken free from the grip of any residual metaphysical Cartesianism. While Descartes and Pessoa share a commitment to the employment of a method of first-personal inquiry, Pessoa rejects Descartes's conclusion: the self is not a metaphysically fundamental substance but is rather something that is grounded in features of fields of experience. Contemporary philosophers of mind are no less hostile to Cartesian souls than is Pessoa and have therefore largely endorsed what has seemed to them to be the only available alternative, that selves are simply bodily human beings. Mark Johnston says, for example, 'What could a self, understood as the denotation of 'I', be? . . . A self need not have anything but biological parts making it up over its lifetime. It need not be, at any time, made up of something less, or more, than the human being.'[1] The full passage reads as a brilliant lesson in the Western history of selfhood:

> The suggestion that 'I' instead picks out a self is a common one, embodied in the very term 'the ego', but the suggestion is usually paired with the idea that a self is 'something less than the whole human being', as it might be a mental substance or mental core of a self-conscious life, the true or primary subject of thought, something that inhabits a human being. We have

---

[1] Johnston, *Surviving Death*, p. 198.

Virtual Subjects, Fugitive Selves: Fernando Pessoa and his Philosophy. Jonardon Ganeri, Oxford University Press (2021). © Jonardon Ganeri. DOI: 10.1093/oso/9780198864684.001.0001

found reason to doubt that a use of 'I' denotes a self in this sense. Just suppose that there are no such selves. Still, 'I' seems to remain a denoting term; for example, 'I am Johnston' still seems to be true in the conceivable scenario in which there are no such selves. Likewise, David Hume looked into himself and found no self, yet Hume successfully uses 'I' and its cognates throughout his very repudiation of such a self. This suggests that the successful use of 'I' carries no such metaphysical commitment to a self. All we had better rely on for uses of 'I' to denote, it seems, are arenas of presence with human or other self-conscious beings at the centers. If we are to resort to selves as the references of various uses of 'I', then we should employ no more than these materials to explain the nature of selves. So, absent persisting mental particulars that lie at the heart of our mental lives, what could a self, understood as the denotation of 'I', be? Drawing on our earlier notion of an arena of presence, a self could be something whose cross-time unity condition was that all the entities that successively constituted it were successively at the center of a given persisting arena of presence. A self, in this sense, need not have anything but biological parts making it up over its lifetime. It need not be, at any time, made up of something less, or more, than the human being.[2]

The one possibility Johnston overlooks in all this is the Pessoan possibility that selves are indices of manners of resonance in arenas of presence.

There is a clear commitment to the conventional view in the writings of Valberg, who insists that it is a human being who is 'the one that I am', and writes that 'perhaps (since they don't exist) we can leave souls out of this'.[3] When he spells out the content of the positional conception of self, he does so by identifying three embodied sorts of centrality. He says,

[W]hen we look into the question of what makes a particular body 'mine', a particular human being 'me', i.e., when we ask about the way of figuring within my horizon by virtue of which a particular human being (human body) is the one at the centre and is thereby 'me' ('mine'), it emerges that the question has not one but three answers, that there are three kinds of centrality. The human being (body) that is 'me' ('mine') is the one that is perceptually present in a unique way (perceptual centrality); is the one

---

[2] Johnston, *Surviving Death*, p. 198.
[3] Valberg, *Dream, Death, and the Self*, pp. 356–27.

Figure 12.1 Ernst Mach, illustration from 'The analysis of the sensations: antimetaphysical', *The Monist* 1 (1890), p. 59.

that is the locus of feeling (centrality of feeling); and is the one whose movements figure as willed (volitional centrality).[4]

That is to say, one is perceptually aware of one's own body as occupying a distinctive position within one's field of view (as in Ernst Mach's famous 'self-portrait': I see my legs stretched out before me; see Figure 12.1);[5] one is aware of one's own body kinaesthetically too, as the kinaesthetic space in which one's own bodily feelings take place (I feel a tingle in my toe); and one is aware of one's own body as the physical object over which one has immediate volitional control (I raise my arm to grasp the pen).

Let me say that when the positional conception is grounded in one or more of these three sorts of embodied centrality the self thereby conceived of is an 'actual subject'.[6] Pessoa sometimes appeals himself to the idea of

---

[4] Valberg, *Dream, Death, and the Self*, p. 271.

[5] Mach, Ernst. 'The analysis of the sensations: antimetaphysical'. *The Monist* 1 (1890), pp. 48–68, at p. 59.

[6] It is possible, at least conceptually, that these three centres should come apart, and then the question 'Where am I?' admits no univocal answer. Daniel Dennett explores this in his Borgesian science-fiction story, 'Where am I?', *Brainstorms*, MIT Press, 1981, pp. 310–23. When there is a separation between the so-called 'field' perspective and 'observer' perspective, for instance in a dream, what constitutes the 'field' perspective is often a display of perceptual centrality, while the 'observer' perspective exhibits volitional centrality.

actual subjects: 'Yes, for a moment I was someone else: in someone else I saw and lived this human and humble joy of existing as an animal in shirtsleeves.'[7] Animalists, who identify the self with the human body, and 'embodied mind' theorists, who argue that all cognition is embodied, affirm not just that there are actual subjects but that there are no other subjects: embodied phenomenology is the only source of phenomenal centrality. Yet, and this is something Valberg himself concedes, the positional conception of self is available even in the absence of an embodied human being at the centre. Valberg's concession is that there can be what he calls an 'emptiness at the centre', cases in which, although the field of sensation has a phenomenal centre, there is no bodily human being around to occupy it: 'We can imagine that within my horizon, within my experience, there is nothing that figures at the centre.... We can, you might say, imagine a standing emptiness at the centre, an experience (horizon) in which the subject position is standingly unoccupied, in which therefore there is no one who is "me"', he says, immediately clarifying that, 'when we speak of "emptiness at the centre", we mean that there is *no human being* at the centre of my horizon.'[8] To say this is, evidently, to acknowledge that there are sources of phenomenal centrality other than those that are due to embodiment. In Part III of this book I will provide a range of concrete examples, but for the time being let me simply note that this is already the case in Valberg's example, 'In my dream, I am X'. Valberg does not tell us much about the mysterious person whom he names, somewhat unrevealingly, 'X'. What we do know is that X is the one at the centre of a field of experience, a field within which another person, JV, is present. I have argued that this is an exact analogue, in dreams, of heteronymic subjectivity, the simulation of a centred field of experience in directed imagination, and so of Pessoa's writing in the first person as Caeiro or Reis or Campos. I do not deny that Pessoa ascribes bodily attributes to his heteronyms—they are not ethereal spirits or Cartesian souls; they have life stories—but the claim that I am making is that the centrality of the fields of experience of which they are at the centre is not explained by those bodily attributes and is not a purely embodied centrality.

Let me call the occupant of a field of experience whose centrality is *not* explained in terms of facts about embodiment a 'virtual subject'. A virtual subject is an abstract entity, and there is a standard way to introduce and define abstract entities of any type. This is the method of definition by abstraction, first proposed by Gottlob Frege, who used it to define numbers

---

[7] *The Book of Disquiet*, #374.
[8] Valberg, *Dream, Death, and the Self*, pp. 355–6, my italics.

on analogy with directions.[9] He said that the direction of a line A is the same as the direction of a second line B just in case the first line is parallel to the second. There is, in any definition by abstraction, an equivalence relation that partitions a domain of entities (here the domain of lines and the relation of being parallel), and an identity relation between a corresponding class of abstract objects (in this case, directions). Let us instead take the domain to be that of sensoria, those landscapes of presence or fields of experience. And let us take the equivalence relation to be that of sameness of manner of resonance. The way to define a virtual subject is then as follows: given any two landscapes of presence, L_1 and L_2, the virtual subject of L_1 is the same as the virtual subject of L_2 if and only if L_1 resonates in the same manner as L_2. And just as, having introduced directions, we can speak about them and say things like 'The wind is from the south-west', so too, having introduced virtual subjects, we can say, for instance, that 'A stone is seen by Caeiro'. So phenomenal centrality, for a virtual subject, has its origin in the for-me-ness of phenomenal experience, and this is but another way of putting the point that for-me-ness is 'the categorical basis of our capacity for first-person thought'.[10] If for-me-ness is the dative of manifestation, then a virtual subject is the derived nominative of manifestation.

This way of introducing and defining virtual subjects sharply differentiates them from Cartesian egos, the 'souls' whose existence is denied as categorically by Pessoa as by Valberg. The reason is that Cartesian egos are not metaphysically dependent on anything, let alone manners of resonance in a field of consciousness. The definition encapsulates Pessoa's claim that 'souls' and the subjective character of the psychological items in fields of experience are metaphysically interdependent: '[Y]ou can't feel in a new way without changing your soul.'[11] The mistake made by the animalist is to think of the centre of a phenomenal field as *merely* a place, one which is contingently filled by different individuals without the way it is filled being dependent on the field itself. One should not, however, think of the subject position simply as an empty hole that a self can be plugged into. That is the point of Brian O'Shaughnessy's denial of what he calls 'the mythical S':

The myth in question takes the following form. It is of a mental existent (which I shall call S), a particular mental 'space' that is of type awareness

[9] Frege, Gottlob. *The Foundations of Arithmetic*, translated by J. L. Austin. Northwestern University Press, 1980, pp. 74–8.
[10] Zahavi and Kriegel, 'For-me-ness: What it is and what it is not', p. 49.
[11] *The Book of Disquiet*, #301.

(in some sense), which coexists with and is distinct from contemporan-
eous experiences. Those experiences relate to that awareness-space, not as
its objects, but as its occupants, and that property enables them to
exist...[There] is something that is closely akin to a psychic space. And
yet as we have just seen in the recent discussion of the mythical S, it cannot be something that, like the space of a canvas or stage, precedes and
outlives its occupants.[12]

Virtual subjects are metaphysically dependent on landscapes of presence;
they are not metaphysically 'distinct' from 'awareness-space'. What makes
Pessoa's heteronymic philosophy of self so fascinating is, precisely, that it
stands as much opposed to both the Cartesian and the animalist pictures as
it does, evidently, to the Humean account of selfhood. My argument in this
and the preceding chapters has been that there exist such interdependencies
between various facets of phenomenality; in a slogan, that to-me-ness with
multiplicity implies in-me-ness and that for-me-ness implies me-ness. Or,
in terms drawn from Pessoa and Valberg, that the positional conception of
self explains the conception of self as meeting-place (Pessoan 'depersonalization'), and the horizonal conception of self explains the conception of self
as heteronym (Pessoan 'simulation'). Having thereby achieved a 'paraphrase'
of Pessoa with the aid of theory drawn from contemporary philosophy of
mind, I will soon, in Part III, apply the new understanding of the nature of
the self thus reached to a series of problems found in the global history of
philosophy. Let me conclude Part II, though, by discussing two additional
Pessoan topics, those of orthonyms and the reality of subjects.

[12] O'Shaughnessy, Brian. *Consciousness and the World*. Oxford, 2002, pp. 285, 288.

13

Orthonyms as Shadow Selves

Pessoa has introduced the term 'heteronym' for the coterie of virtual subjects whose identity he variously assumes. Within this group there is one whose name is 'Fernando Pessoa': 'The strangest case is that of Fernando Pessoa, who doesn't exist, strictly speaking.'[1] In using his own name in this way Pessoa does not intend to refer to himself as the biological human being who lives at Rua Coelho da Rocha, 16. Rather, 'Fernando Pessoa' is here an orthonym, bearing the same name as Fernando Pessoa and standing in a unique relationship to him. 'Fernando Pessoa's writings', says Pessoa, speaking of himself in the third person, 'belong to two categories of works, which we may call orthonymic and heteronymic. The heteronymic works of Fernando Pessoa have been produced by (so far) three people's names—Alberto Caeiro, Ricardo Reis, and Álvaro de Campos...If these three individuals are more or less real than Fernando Pessoa himself is a metaphysical problem that the latter—not privy to the secret of the gods and therefore ignorant of what really is—will never be able to solve.'[2]

This very 'metaphysical problem' comes up as a topic of conversation among the heteronyms themselves. Álvaro de Campos recalls the following conversation with his master Alberto Caeiro:

> One of the most interesting conversations with my master Caeiro was the one in Lisbon where everyone in the group was present and we ended up discussing the concept of Reality....[At one point] Fernando Pessoa turned to Caeiro. 'Tell me this,' he said, pointing his cigarette: 'How do you regard dreams? Are they real or not?' 'I regard dreams as I regard shadows,' answered Caeiro unexpectedly with his usual divine quickness. 'A shadow is real, but it's less real than a stone. A dream is real—otherwise it wouldn't be a dream—but it's less real than a thing.'...'And what do you call a stone that you see in a dream?' asked Fernando, smiling. 'I call it a dream,'

---

[1] 'Notes for the memory of my master Caeiro', in *Selected Prose*, p. 49.
[2] [Bibliographical summary], in *A Little Larger*, p. 3.

Virtual Subjects, Fugitive Selves: Fernando Pessoa and his Philosophy. Jonardon Ganeri,
Oxford University Press (2021). © Jonardon Ganeri.
DOI: 10.1093/oso/9780198864684.001.0001

answered my master Caeiro. 'I call it a dream of a stone.'...'Why do you say "of a stone"? Why do you employ the word "stone"?' 'For the same reason that you, when you see my picture, say "That's Caeiro" and don't mean that it's me in the flesh.' We all broke out laughing. 'I see and I give up,' said Fernando, laughing with the rest of us.[3]

Assuming the heteronym Campos, Pessoa is imagining a conversation between himself-as-Campos, his other heteronyms, and 'Fernando Pessoa'. In the report it is Campos who occupies the subject position, while the one called 'Fernando Pessoa' comes across as an aesthete who lives in a world of ideas with a 'relentlessly intellectualized sensibility, inattentively keen attention, cold self-analysis.'[4] The report exhibits, therefore, exactly the same structure as Valberg's dream, Pessoa imagining a scenario in which he is Campos (and so he might have said, 'In the story, I was Campos') and not Fernando Pessoa, who is nevertheless present as a distinct conversant. We are not to fall into error by presuming that 'Fernando Pessoa', as the name is used within this report, refers to the human being who penned the text, for it is clear that when Pessoa writes, here and elsewhere, about someone called 'Fernando Pessoa' he is employing an orthonym, and doing so precisely because within the imagined scenario he is not Fernando Pessoa (it is not Fernando Pessoa who is the one at the centre; it is Álvaro de Campos). So, too, when Valberg says, 'In my dream I was X, not JV', the name 'JV' figures as an orthonym, and is not being used to make a simple reference to Valberg, the dreaming human subject.

An orthonym, like a heteronym, is a virtual subject, but it is one which stands in a distinguished relationship with a simulating subject. The concept is best understood by way of a genealogical explanation. An orthonym is a virtual subject whose existence is due to an act of displacement, namely the transference of a simulating subject's way of feeling when that subject has undergone depersonalization. This is the mechanism Pessoa himself describes when he says that 'the human author of these books has no personality of his own. Whenever he feels a personality well up inside he quickly realizes that this new being, though similar, is distinct from him— an intellectual son, perhaps, with inherited characteristics, but also with differences that make him someone else.'[5] The 'intellectual son' who is the

---

[3] 'Notes for the memory of my master Caeiro', in *Selected Prose*, pp. 43–6.
[4] 'Notes for the memory of my master Caeiro', in *Selected Prose*, p. 50.
[5] [Aspects], in *Selected Prose*, p. 2.

orthonym 'Fernando Pessoa' is a virtual subject who has inherited Pessoa's non-, or pre-, heteronymic 'personality'. Recall here Saramago's vivid analogy, of Pessoa seeing in a mirror the successive images of his heteronyms—when the last image to appear is that of his own face, it is now no longer he himself he can see, but rather Bernardo Soares, his semi-heteronym.[6] Pessoa says that Bernardo Soares is only semi-heteronymic 'because his personality, although not my own, doesn't differ from my own but is a mere mutilation of it. He's me without my rationalism and emotions. His prose is the same as mine, except for certain formal restraint that reason imposes on my own writing.'[7] Indeed, the name 'Bernardo Soares' is as much a semi-orthonym as a semi-heteronym, being a mere mutilation of the letters which comprise the name 'Fernando Pessoa'. Giorgio Agamben identifies the same genealogical mechanism when, describing heteronymic simulation as a process of 'subjectification' and Pessoan depersonalization as one of 'desubjectification', he writes that:

> it is worth examining this incomparable phenomenology of heteronymic depersonalization. Not only does each new subjectification (the appearance of Alberto Caeiro) imply a desubjectification. At the same time, each desubjectification also implies a resubjectification: the return of Fernando Pessoa…A new poetic consciousness, something like a genuine *ēthos* of poetry, begins once Fernando Pessoa, having survived his own depersonalization, returns to a self who both is and is no longer the first subject.[8]

Exactly so: in necessitating an inner displacement of one's way of feeling, it is the depersonalized awareness of oneself, the awareness of oneself as fugitive, which is the condition of possibility of one's orthonym. In a later chapter, we will find the idea so well expressed by Agamben as the orthonymic return 'to a self who both is and is no longer the first subject' explored with great sophistication in a classical Daoist masterpiece, the *Zhuangzi*.

Pessoa's description of an orthonym as an 'intellectual son' echoes what in antiquity used to go by the name of *syzygos* or 'yoke-mate', thought to be one's divine double. As Charles Stang points out, this premodern notion involves a vertical relationship, and that is what distinguishes it from

---

[6] Saramago, José. *The Notebook*, translated by Amanda Hopkinson and Daniel Hahn. London, Verso, 2010, p. 25.

[7] Letter to Adolfo Casais Monteiro, 13 January 1935. In *Selected Prose*, pp. 258–9.

[8] Agamben, Giorgio. *Remnants of Auschwitz: The Witness and the Archive*. Zone Books, 1999, p. 119.

modern explorations of the doppelgänger or double, where the relationship is a horizontal one:

> The double is not a divine, vertical, visitor, but more often a threat on the horizontal plane—someone who poses a danger to the protagonist, per-haps with the threat that the image might replace the archetype...If modernity seems exercised by the threat of a menacing doppelgänger, a horizontal double, then late antiquity seems equally exercised by the promise of a divine counterpart, a vertical double.[9]

Whether as doppelgänger or *syzygos*, whether horizontal or vertical, the mechanism in play is that of orthonymy, the threatened displacement of oneself from the subject position by an imposter who is oneself. When the counterpart is divine, it is perhaps one's better, truer, self, of which one is merely a mortal shadow: 'What you are you do not see, what you see is your shadow,' wrote Rabindranath Tagore, the famous Bengali poet whose poems Pessoa possessed.[10]

It is more common in works of fiction for authors to have the protagonist speak in the first person, while the thoughts and actions of their double are described instead in the third person. Rather than an explicit orthonym there is often then a bare use of the third-person pronoun. There is, typic-ally, little effort made to provide the double with any specific characteriza-tion, the implication being that the reader can infer the double's personality from that of the protagonist. In the *nivola*, a genre named and pioneered by Miguel de Unamuno, the author *entirely* dispenses with plot and character-ization; as Íngrid Vendell Ferran explains, it is a literary form which 'is much more interested in the monologues and dialogues between the char-acters than in the descriptions of time and space or in plot development.'[11] The narrator of Unamuno's story, *The Novel of Don Sandalio, Chessplayer*, written in 1930, is interested only in a figure he refers to as 'my Don

---

[9] Stang, Charles. *Our Divine Double*. Harvard, 2016, p. 12.
[10] Tagore, Rabindranath. *Stray Birds*. Macmillan & Co., 1917, §18. Pessoa owned at least two works of Tagore: Tagore, Rabindranath. *Gītāñjali and Fruit-gathering*, with an introduction by W. B. Yeats. Leipzig, 1922; Tagore, Rabindranath. *Poems*. London, 1925. He has underlined the *Gītāñjali's* first sentence, 'Thou hast made me endless, such is thy pleasure / This frail vessel thou emptiest again and again, and fillest it ever with fresh life.' In the marginalia, he rendered another of Tagore's poems into Portuguese.
[11] Ferran, Íngrid Vendrell. 'Narrative fiction as philosophical exploration: A case study of self-envy and akrasia'. In *Literature as Thought Experiment? Perspectives from Philosophy and Literary Studies*, edited by Bornmüller, Falk, Franzen, Johannes, and Lessau, Mathis. Brill, 2019, pp. 123–37.

Sandalio': 'This Don Sandalio, not the one who plays chess with me in the Casino, but the other, the one *he* has imposed on my innermost soul, my Don Sandalio, follows me everywhere now, and I even dream of him, and almost suffer with him.'[12] Deftly employing a panoply of tropes of dreams, shadows and mirrors to describe the relationship between the narrator and 'his' Don Sandalio, it is with this assessment that the novel ends:

> And now I begin to remember all over again, to recall and to reconstruct certain obscure dreams I dreamt along the way: they are shadows which do not appear in front of one or come alongside, but are like those which evanesce into the distance of dim tarnished mirrors. On returning home some nights *I would meet a human shadow falling across my inner awareness*; it would project itself into my dormant consciousness and rouse it strangely; and the shadow would then lower its head, as if to avoid recognition.... That shadow I see before me now, off the beaten track, in retrotime, walking by with head bowed—his? or mine?—could it be Don Sandalio...?[13]

This is a fine description of the orthonymic double, a shadow of oneself within one's imagination and awareness. An orthonym is indeed a shadow self, oneself transformed into another I.

A brief story by Jorge Luis Borges, *August 25, 1983*, affords us another superb illustration. Our protagonist, writing in the first person, enters a familiar hotel, only to find that someone has already signed himself in under the name 'Jorge Luis Borges' and is already installed in his room: 'I tried the door; it opened at my touch. The overhead light still burned. In the pitiless light, I came face to face with myself. There, in the narrow iron bed—older, withered, and very pale—lay I.'[14] 'How odd,' it was saying, 'we are two and yet we are one. But then nothing is odd in dreams... [for] still I dream these dreams of my double...that tiresome subject I got from Stevenson and mirrors.'[15] The doubling in this story is a diachronic

---

[12] Unamuno, Miguel de. *The novel of Don Sandalio, chess player.* In *Fictions*, vol. 7 of the *Selected Works of Miguel de Unamuno*, translated by Anthony Kerrigan. Princeton, 1976, pp. 183–226, at. p.197.

[13] Unamuno, *The novel of Don Sandalio, chess player*, pp. 218–9, my italics.

[14] Borges, Jorge Luis. *25 August 1983.* In *Collected Fictions*, translated by Andrew Hurley. Penguin, 1999, pp. 489–93. A similar example is to be found in Giorgio Manganelli's *La Notte* (Milan, 1996). Manganelli speaks not of orthonymy but of 'homopseudonymy', the use of one's own name as a pseudonym, a mask.

[15] Borges, *25 August 1983*, p. 490.

doubling, an encounter between two temporal phases of oneself. The elder Borges now foretells what the younger one has to look forward to, which he does by remembering his own past. In this story, 'Borges' the orthonym is an intellectual son but a temporal father. 'Don't you realize that the first thing to find out is whether there is only one man dreaming, or two men dreaming each other,' the orthonym is given to say.[16]

It is hard to know, in stories like these, whether the protagonist or their double is the more real. Indeed, that is a large part of their point: to force us to think about what the reality of subjects consists in. In the final section of this Part, I will review Pessoa's fascinating, if sometimes opaque, ideas about this problem, the 'metaphysical problem that I—not privy to the secret of the gods and therefore ignorant of what really is—will never be able to solve'.

---

[16] Borges, *25 August 1983*, p. 492.

14

The Reality of Subjects

'Do I, who make you exist in me, have more real life than you [...]?'[1] Is a virtual subject any 'less real', whatever that might mean, than the subject who simulates it in themselves? Pessoa often expresses hesitation in his ability to tell what is more real and what is less, the actual or the virtual, veridical experience or dream, fact or fiction: 'The author of these books cannot affirm that all these different and well-defined personalities who have incorporeally passed through his soul don't exist, for he does not know what it means to exist, nor whether Hamlet or Shakespeare is more real, or truly real,'[2] he says. 'The only problem is that of reality, as insoluble as it is alive. What do I know about the difference between a tree and a dream? I can touch the tree; I know that I have the dream. What is all this really?'[3] 'I'm so used to feeling what's false as true, and what I dream as vividly as what I see, that I've lost the human distinction—false, I believe—between truth and falsehood.'[4]

At other times Pessoa offers something like a criterion to distinguish the imaginary from the empirical. Imagined entities are 'one-sided' in a manner actual entities are not: 'The things we dream have just one side. We can't walk around them to see what's on the other side. The problem with the things of life is that we can look at them from all sides.'[5] Pessoa immediately goes on to claim that subjects belong within the category of the imagined: 'The things we dream have, like our own souls, only the side that we see.' Again, 'We are phantoms made of lies, shadows of illusions, and our life is hollow on both the outside and the inside.'[6] To put the matter in the terms of our preceding discussion, this is simply to stress that subjects are metaphysically dependent on fields of experience.

There is, in all these remarks, a rejection of a certain, classical approach to thinking about existence, the one which, beginning with Plato, invites us to draw a distinction between appearance and reality. Reality is the single

---

[1] 'Peristyle', *The Book of Disquiet*, p. 445.   [2] [Aspects], in *Selected Prose*, p. 2.
[3] *The Book of Disquiet*, #378.   [4] *The Book of Disquiet*, #157.
[5] *The Book of Disquiet*, #346.   [6] *The Book of Disquiet*, #364.

Virtual Subjects, Fugitive Selves: Fernando Pessoa and his Philosophy. Jonardon Ganeri,
Oxford University Press (2021). © Jonardon Ganeri.
DOI: 10.1093/oso/9780198864684.001.0001

domain of what there is; all else is mere appearance, fabrications of the mind, merely intentional. Pessoa, however, putting the issue in terms of what is more real and what is less, instead introduces a layered conception of reality in which there are distinct domains of reals and some sort of ordering among them. I have hinted several times that we can employ a concept from contemporary metaphysics, the concept of grounding, to reformulate Pessoa's idea.[7] Grounding is the idea that the existence of one sort of entity is 'due to' that of another, that these entities exist because of, or in virtue of, the existence of those others. It is a metaphysician's term for the 'because' in Pessoa's assertion that 'everything that exists perhaps exists because something else exists.'[8] Suppose that, dissatisfied with the claim that shadows are mere appearance, one wants to say instead that a shadow does really exist, but that it is 'less real' than the thing of which it is a shadow. The concept of grounding is what one needs to say this: the shadow only exists in virtue of that which casts it, the entity which constitutes its grounds for being. Its existence is dependent, in a certain sense, on the existence of something else. Notice that it does not follow that reality as such is a concept that admits of degree, and the talk of things being 'more real' or 'less real' ('A shadow is real, but it's less real than a stone') is, from this perspective, a somewhat metaphorical way of saying that some things exist because other things do. An entity is 'more real' in the sense that it is more fundamental, 'less real' if less fundamental, the most fundamental of all being something, if there is any such thing, that is not grounded in anything else.

Pessoa's view, then, seems to be that subjects of experience are grounded (and therefore are not Cartesian souls), and that the grounding of both actual and virtual subjects is the same. The intuitive view that unsimulated subjects ground simulated ones, that Shakespeare is 'more real' than Hamlet, is regarded as deeply suspicious if not rejected outright. To say this is, in effect, to say that the metaphor of a shadow only takes us so far, and is ultimately an inadequate one. One reason the metaphor breaks down is that there is no such thing as a shadow's shadow: shadows do not themselves cast shadows. We have, however, encountered no reason to think that a

---

[7] Correia, Fabrice, and Schnieder, Benjamin, eds. *Metaphysical Grounding: Understanding the Structure of Reality.* Cambridge, 2012.

[8] *The Book of Disquiet*, #441. The full passage introduces additional complexities: 'Everything that exists perhaps exists because something else exists. Nothing is, everything coexists—perhaps that's how it really is. I feel I wouldn't exist right now—or at least wouldn't exist in the way I'm existing, with this present consciousness of myself, which, because it is consciousness and present, is entirely me in this moment—if that lamp weren't shining somewhere over there, a useless lighthouse with a specious advantage of height.'

heteronym cannot itself assume a heteronym: that a subject which is itself simulated cannot simulate another.[9] Metaphors of mirrors are an improvement in this respect, for it does seem possible to speak of a reflection itself having a reflection, in the case where there are mirrors in parallel, even if the more correct description would refer instead to primary and secondary reflections of the object itself. A mirror image, if treated not as mere appearance but as something real if 'less real', is grounded in that which the mirror reflects. Unamuno and Borges both, as we have just seen, prefer to think of doubles and orthonyms in terms of metaphors of shadows and mirrors.

Metaphors drawn from the world of virtual-reality gaming, meanwhile, with its talk of simulacra, avatars, and so on, are arguably helpful, but they too have limits. A heteronym is a simulated subject, and simulated subjects are not simulacra. When, in the conversation I discussed above, Pessoa, assuming the heteronym Campos, writes of a conversation between the gang of heteronyms, Campos, insofar as he is the one who occupies the subject position, is not a mere avatar of Pessoa in this imagined, simulated scenario. At best one might describe the simulated scenario as one in which there are multiple avatars of Pessoa in conversation with one another, but the crucial datum this fails to capture is that each of the heteronyms, even if now presented in the third-person, has the capacity to serve in the subject position, to be the one at the centre of a simulation.

The imaginary conversation itself concerns different views about the reality of dream objects, views which are clearly distinguished and assigned to different participants in the conversation. The orthonym 'Fernando Pessoa' is given to take the position that words refer directly in any context, even dream contexts, to specific actual things. Presumably, he would say the same about the subject within the dream, the one at the centre of the dream landscape of sensation. Valberg, to compare, says:

> In my dream my daughter was seated next to me. So my daughter was in my dream. And by 'my daughter' I mean (who else?) my daughter, the girl in school about two miles from this café...If we can handle the superficial puzzlement about my daughter, or this cafe, being in a dream of mine, there should be no special problem about me—the human being that I am, the one who dreamed those past dreams—being in such a dream.[10]

---

[9] See the later chapter, 'Dreams inside Dreams'.

[10] Valberg, *Dream, Death, and the Self*, pp. 61–2. Valberg's claim, here, is that 'my daughter' refers directly and dream contexts are extensional, and that the positional use of 'I' is one of direct reference.

Alberto Caeiro, though, does not find the puzzle superficial, and adopts the different view that the same name is used systematically to refer to different entities in different contexts: 'I call it a dream of a stone.'... 'Why do you say "of a stone"? Why do you employ the word "stone"?' 'For the same reason that you, when you see my picture, say "That's Caeiro" and don't mean that it's me in the flesh.' Caeiro has observed that we typically name representations after the objects they represent. Perhaps we can read the conversation as an allegory for the progress of Pessoa's own thought, from pre-heteronymic rationalism to the more complex implications of heteronymy?[11] The subject-within-a-dream is neither identical to the dreaming subject nor a mere avatar: it is an echo, an orthonym; it is a simulation, a heteronym.

What we need is a way to make sense of the idea that subjects of experience which are simulated in imagination are no 'less real' than the subjects of experience in everyday life. There have, indeed, been studies which suggest that there is a functional equivalence in the two cases. For example, Tamar Gendler identifies a phenomenon which she calls 'source-indifference' and defines thus: 'Certain features of our mental architecture are source-indifferent, in the sense that they process internally and externally generated content in similar ways.'[12] Results from studies of visual and motor imagery strongly indicate that behavioural outcomes are, in many cases, indifferent to their origin, whether it be in imaginative or in perceptual machinery. One way the source-indifference shows up is in what Gendler calls 'imaginative contagion', that is, 'cases where merely imagining or pretending P has effects that we would expect only believing or perceiving P to have.'[13] Gendler notes that contagion is present in cases of visual imagination and the activation of social categories, and also that there is affective contagion (a child pretending there is a bear in the closet will hesitate before opening the door). The type of imagination Pessoa concerns himself with is of a more complex sort: the enactive heteronymic simulation of a virtual subject. Yet his claim that virtual subjects are, in some sense, 'just as real' can itself be understood as a variety of source-indifference, and the point would then be that it is of no significance how a subject is generated: '[T]he process that thrusts a

---

[11] A move, perhaps, away from the view that 'I' is a simple indexical to an appreciation that it has positional and horizonal uses, and away from direct reference theories in the light of the complexities introduced by orthonymy and heteronymy. Animalists like Valberg, it would seem, wish to resist the second move even while making the first.

[12] Gendler, Tamar. 'Imaginative contagion'. In her *Intuition, Imagination, & Philosophical Methodology*. Oxford, 2010, pp. 238–54, at p. 238.

[13] Gendler, 'Imaginative contagion', p. 238.

certain aspect of the world or the figure of a dream into a more-than-real reality also thrusts emotions and thoughts into the more-than-real sphere...I haven't really fled from life, in the sense of seeking a softer bed for my soul; I've merely changed lives, finding in my dreams the same objectivity that I found in life.'[14] The distinction between actual and virtual subjects consists only in the respective source of phenomenal centrality, and their status as subjects is indifferent as to the origin of the experiential field's centredness. For Pessoa the most important source-indifferent behavioural outcome consists, of course, in the composition of poetry, at which each of his primary heteronyms excels, as indeed does the elusive figure known only as 'Fernando Pessoa'.

---

[14] 'Milky way', *The Book of Disquiet*, pp. 433–4. Also, *A Little Larger*, p. 67.

PART III
PESSOA PROVOKED

15

Uncentred Minds

I began by presenting Pessoa's remarkable philosophy of self more or less in his own words. I then drew on available materials in contemporary philosophy of mind to paraphrase his theory and in so doing to provide rather more precise definitions of key Pessoan notions, as well as to formulate a solution to the enigma of heteronymy. As I will now go on to demonstrate, some of the most puzzling and fascinating reflections about the philosophy of self in the global history of philosophy can better be understood if we apply Pessoa's insights to them. One might be forgiven, indeed, for thinking that Pessoa has thoroughly explored the outer reaches of subjective possibility. Yet, as I will also show, it will turn out that we must revise and extend Pessoa's theory in light of the challenges some of these puzzles pose.

My cases will be drawn from thinkers from the Indian, Buddhist, Chinese, and Persian worlds, as well as from sources contemporary with Pessoa himself. These puzzles bear directly on the central question addressed in a Pessoan philosophy of self: what metaphysical grounding relations are in play for individual subjects of experience? In virtue of what, because of what, in dependence on what, do conscious subjects exist? It is not my intention to enter into a study of the influence of non-European thought on Pessoa,[1] but let me anyway note that Pessoa's library is surprisingly rich in its holdings on non-European philosophy. His copies of Victor Henry's *Les Littératures de l'Inde: sancrit, pâli, prâcrit* and George Mead's *Quests Old and New* are both thoroughly annotated, the former including a survey of the philosophy of the six Hindu schools with even a reconstruction of the Nyāya

---

[1] See Pizarro, Jerónimo, Ferrari, Patricio, and Cardiello, Antonio. 'Os Orientes de Fernando Pessoa'. *Cultura Entre Culturas* 3 (2011), pp. 148–85; Cardiello, Antonio. 'Os Orientes de Fernando Pessoa: adenda'. *Pessoa Plural* 10 (2016), pp. 128–85. Some of Pessoa's writings about India are discussed in Braga, Druarte Drumond. 'Um roteiro pessoano sobre a Índia'. *Pessoa Plural* 10 (2016), pp. 11–36, and his theosophical translations in Mota, Pedro da. 'A Caminho do Oriente: apontamentos de Pessoa sobre Teosofia e espiritualidades da Índia'. *Pessoa Plural* 10 (2016), pp. 230–51. See also my 'Pessoa's imaginary India'. In *Fernando Pessoa & Philosophy*, edited by Bartholomew Ryan, Giovanbattista Tusa, and Antonio Cardiello. Roman & Littlefield, 2021.

Virtual Subjects, Fugitive Selves: Fernando Pessoa and his Philosophy. Jonardon Ganeri, Oxford University Press (2021). © Jonardon Ganeri.
DOI: 10.1093/oso/9780198864684.001.0001

'syllogism,' the latter containing a careful summary of Shwe Zan Aung's translation of the *Abhidhammattha-saṅgaha*, with an exact description of Theravāda philosophy of mind. Also heavily annotated is his copy of Ella Fletcher's *The Law of the Rhythmic Breath*, which contains an extensive account of the principles of the Sāṃkhya-Yoga system. Pessoa owned several works of South Asian literature in translation: the plays of Kālidāsa, including *Śakuntalā*; the *Kāma-sūtra* in the French translation of E. Lamairesse; the *Gītāñjali* of Rabindranath Tagore with an introduction by W. B. Yeats, and another anthology of Tagore's poetry. Pessoa, we may also note, spent his early life in Durban, living there for a decade from 1896, a town at which Mahatma Gandhi had arrived three years earlier when he was already honing his skills as a civil-rights activist. Pessoa would later write, 'Mahatma Gandhi is the only truly great figure in the world today.'[2]

In this chapter I will explore the relationship between Pessoa's philosophy of self and Buddhism. I begin, somewhat obtusely, with the brilliant French philosopher Simone Weil (1909–43), a contemporary of Pessoa but someone of whom he certainly had never heard. 'To empty ourselves of our false divinity, to deny ourselves, to give up being the centre of the world in imagination, to discern that all points in the world are equally centres and that the true centre is outside the world, this is to consent to the rule of mechanical necessity in matter and of free choice at the centre of each soul,'[3] she writes. Weil's ethics is one of 'self-emptying', a stripping away (*dépouillement*) of the 'I'. 'To say "I" is to lie,' she says.[4] One way to read these remarks, by no means the only way, is as directed against the positional use of 'I', against the deployment in thought and speech of a positional conception of self. One should abandon forms of self-consciousness that are grounded in one's thinking of oneself as the one at the centre of a landscape of sensation. This moral prescription demands of one that one reorder one's mind in such a way as to eliminate any centre-periphery structure in one's field of experience. If Pessoa said that 'the geography of our consciousness of reality is an endless complexity of irregular coasts, low and high mountains, and myriad lakes,'[5] the challenge now is to comprehend how the phenomenal field be so structured and not have a centre, not have anything to whom the psychological items defer.

---

[2] Quoted in Cardiello, 'Os Orientes de Fernando Pessoa: adenda', p.167.
[3] Weil, Simone. *Waiting for God*, translated by Emma Craufurd. HarperCollins, 2009, p. 100.
[4] Weil, Simone. *First and Last Notebooks*, translated by Richard Rees. Oxford, 1970, p. 132.
[5] *The Book of Disquiet*, #338.

Is it a genuine possibility to experience an 'all this' without the psychological field displaying the sort of structure that would put one in a position
to think of oneself as being at its centre? We have already argued that it is
simply part of the grammar of consciousness that any given psychological
item has an addressee. So what the proposal must amount to is that, in the
uncentred mind, there is no common centre to which every psychological
item is addressed. With respect to such a mind the positional conception
would have no purchase. To such a mind there would be no positional way
of thinking of itself, and so no positional self. I could not truly say, using 'I'
positionally, that 'I am...', and if I were to utter these words I would simply
be engaging, says Weil, in a self-pejorative slur.

The possibility of imagining a mind for which the positional conception
of self is inoperative is not one Pessoa considers. I think he would have
regarded such a mind as profoundly disordered, perhaps as similar to the
phenomenological state of someone suffering from Tourette's syndrome, as
so brilliantly depicted by Oliver Sacks in *The Man who Mistook his Wife
for a Hat*:

> Lacking the normal, protective barriers of inhibition, the normal, organic-
> ally determined boundaries of self, the Touretter's ego is subject to a life-
> long bombardment. He is beguiled, assailed, by impulses from within and
> without. There is a physiological, an existential, almost a theological pres-
> sure upon the soul of the Touretter – whether it can be held whole and
> sovereign, or whether it will be taken over, possessed and dispossessed, by
> every immediacy and impulse. Hume, as we have noted, wrote: 'I venture
> to affirm...that [we] are nothing but a bundle or collection of different
> sensations, succeeding one another with inconceivable rapidity, and in a
> perpetual flux and movement.' Thus, for Hume, personal identity is a fic-
> tion – we do not exist, we are but a consecution of sensations, or percep-
> tions. This is clearly not the case with a normal human being, because he
> owns his own perceptions. They are not a mere flux, but his own, united
> by an abiding individuality or self. But what Hume describes may be pre-
> cisely the case for a being as unstable as a super-Touretter, whose life is, to
> some extent, a consecution of random or convulsive perceptions and
> motions, a phantasmagoric fluttering *with no centre* or sense. To this
> extent he is a 'Humean' rather than a human being.[6]

---

[6] Sacks, Oliver. *The Man who Mistook his Wife for a Hat and Other Clinical Tales.* New York
1990, p. 124; my italics.

Weil's view, however, is certainly not that we should reduce ourselves to merely Humean beings. Her idea is that there is indeed a mental activity which gives unity and wholeness to the uncentred mind, namely the activity of attending to the real: 'The soul empties itself of all its own contents in order to receive into itself the being it is looking at, just as it is, in all its truth. Only he who is capable of attention can do this.'[7] 'Attention alone—that attention which is so full that the "I" disappears—is required of me. I have to deprive all that I call "I" of the light of my attention and turn it on to that which cannot be conceived.'[8] For Weil, it is precisely such contact with reality as attention makes possible which holds the uncentred mind together, preventing its content being 'a phantasmagoric fluttering with no sense'. The uncentred mind would thus be a sort of conformal and aperspectival *map* of reality, standing in correspondence with the world without any privileged perspectival point. It would have as much order as the world has, no more and no less. Pessoa himself continues, if ironically,

> The geography of our consciousness of reality is an endless complexity of irregular coasts, low and high mountains, and myriad lakes. And if I ponder too much, I see it all as a kind of map, like that of the *Pays du Tendre* or *Gulliver's Travels*, a fantasy of exactitude inscribed in an ironic and fanciful book for the amusement of superior beings.[9]

What would it be like for an uncentred mind to experience the world? Perhaps immersive installations like the infinity rooms of the brilliant conceptual artist Yayoi Kusama are an attempt to capture the phenomenology. In these rooms the mirrored surfaces of the walls create the impression of endless repetition, an infinite three-dimensional matrix in which the viewer no longer occupies a privileged viewing position. These immersive installations grew out of Kusama's earlier infinity net painting, which 'has the effect somewhat of a net floating on the ocean, a veil shimmering across reality'.[10] Kusama, significantly for our purposes, describes them as 'paintings that ignored composition and had no centres. The monotony produced by their repetitive patterns bewildered the viewer, while their hypnotic serenity

---

[7] Weil, *Waiting for God*, p. 65.
[8] Weil, Simone. *Gravity and Grace*, translated by Emma Crawford and Mario von der Ruhr. London: Routledge, 2002, p. 118.
[9] *The Book of Disquiet*, #338.
[10] Kusama, Yayoi. *Infinity Net: The Autobiography of Yayoi Kusama*. Tate Publications, 2011, 'A successful debut'.

drew the spirit into a vertigo of nothingness…' And she relates this telling anecdote: 'One day an artist who had found success in Paris and become renowned around the world called at my studio. This ebullient Frenchman…said "Why don't you read Kant and Hegel? There's so much greatness out there! How can you repeat these meaningless exercises, day and night, for years?" But I was under the spell of the polka dot nets…'[11] I wonder if this artist understood, perhaps only unconsciously, the challenge presented to Enlightenment philosophy of self by Kusama's art? For there is no room for German idealism's celebration of the individual ego in her conception of mind: 'By obliterating one's individual self,' she says, 'one returns to the infinite universe,' a sentence that could easily have been uttered by Simone Weil herself.

This is all a far cry from Pessoan depersonalization, which in his hands means the self-consciousness of the fugitive self, a type of self-awareness available only to someone who *can* use 'I' positionally, because it is the awareness that the occupation of the central position is always only contingent. If in Kusama, who was clinically diagnosed with depersonalization disorder, the phenomenology of depersonalization expresses itself in centrelessness, for Pessoa, on the other hand, the phenomenology is rather that of the fugitive. Pessoa does say, as we have seen, 'I am nothing—just an abstract centre of impersonal sensations.'[12] Yet this is the idea of there being potentially an emptiness at the centre, the idea, in other words, that the centre position may go unoccupied, the very possibility Valberg admits of when he says, 'We can imagine that within my horizon, within my experience, there is nothing that figures at the centre….We can, you might say, imagine a standing emptiness at the centre, an experience (horizon) in which the subject position is standingly unoccupied, in which therefore there is no one who is "me".'[13] Although there is now no one at the centre, the conception of an abstract centre continues here to serve as a placeholder. The positional use of 'I' is still available to such a thinker, it is simply that, like 'the present king of France', there happens to be nothing which the descriptive demonstrative picks out.

Such a concept of an emptiness at the centre is evidently very different from Weil's idea of centrelessness. Weil's ethics of self-emptying is an injunction not merely to leave the position at the centre unoccupied but so to restructure the

---

[11] Kusama, *Infinity Net*, 'Taking my stand with a single polka dot'.
[12] *The Book of Disquiet*, #208.
[13] Valberg, J. J. *Dream, Death, and the Self*. Princeton, 2007, p. 355–6.

landscape of sensation that there is no centre position at all. What I am at pains to stress is that the uncentred mind *is* ordered, ordered because it stands in an aperspectival mapping relation with the layout of the real world.

With these distinctions in mind, what more can we say of the mind of Alberto Caeiro, Caeiro who 'values immediacy in knowing and detachment in meditation that do not involve conscious thought',[14] who lives 'without thinking about it':

> I'm a keeper of sheep.
> The sheep are my thoughts.
> And each thought is a sensation.
> I think with my eyes and my ears
> And with my hands and feet
> And with my nose and mouth.
> To think a flower is to see it and smell it,
> And to eat a fruit is to know its meaning.[15]

Again,

> I say of the stone, 'It's a stone'.
> I say of the plant, 'It's a plant'.
> I say of myself, 'It's me'.
> And I say no more. What more is there to say?[16]

Caeiro's manner of experience is immediate, direct, and non-conceptual. Each thing is seen as it is, without mediation or interpretation. It is as Caeiro that Pessoa writes,

> If the soul were more real
> Than the outer world, as you, philosopher, say it is,
> Then why was the outer world given to me as reality's
>   prototype?[17]

[14] Jackson, David. *Adverse Genres in Fernando Pessoa*. New York: Oxford University Press, 2010, pp. 130–1.

[15] *A Little Larger than the Entire Universe: Selected Poems*, edited and translated by Richard Zenith. Penguin, 2006, p. 23. The name 'Caeiro' is no accident, being a play on that of Pessoa's friend Mário de Sá-Carneiro, 'Carneiro' being Portuguese for 'sheep'.

[16] *A Little Larger*, p. 79.

[17] *A Little Larger*, p. 67.

Alberto Caeiro is the Master, someone whose phenomenological style is to 'feel the reality of things' and whose literary style is to make poetry from the absence of thought or sentiment. His creed is one of pure sensationism: sensation is all and thought a disease; things must be felt *as they are*. This certainly echoes a general Buddhist emphasis on seeing things just as they are (*yathā-bhūtam*), and perhaps there is some truth in the suggestion that Caeiro is a Buddhist heteronym. The question is a complicated one because there are as many different schools of Buddhist philosophy as there are ways to understand the meaning of the Buddhist 'no self' (*anātman*) thesis. On one understanding it indeed means emptiness at the centre of my experience, an interpretation of Buddhist 'no self' that, as we have seen, does not require the rejection of the positional conception of self. That is actually how things stand with one of the first schools of Buddhist interpretation, the Abhidharma, whose understanding gained sway in the lands of Theravāda Buddhism. These Buddhist philosophers describe with great care the structuring of the field of experience, and they reject the idea that there is anything like an agent self at its centre. While they have little to say about virtual subjects, and do not anticipate the idea of heteronymy, they are comfortable with the idea that there is a phenomenal centre position and it is empty.[18]

There are places in Pessoa's writing where something like the Theravāda interpretation of 'no self' is countenanced, along with the idea that the self is at best a construct out of impersonal sensations: 'I am nothing—just an abstract centre of impersonal sensations.'[19] Yet it would be a mistake to say that Caeiro is a *Theravāda* heteronym, for the simple reason that concepts do have an important role in the Theravāda understanding of the structure of the field of experience, where they are described as 'labels' (*saññā*), and a proto-conceptual process of labelling is said to accompany every moment of conscious experience.[20] It was the American mystic Thomas Merton who, as the first translator of Pessoa into English, put forward a different conjecture, that Caeiro is a *Zen* heteronym, finding in Caeiro's poems a resonance of the Japanese idea of *satori*, which for him signified 'the unfolding of a new world hitherto unperceived in the confusion of a dualistic mind...a sort of inner perception—not the perception, indeed, of a single individual

---

[18] See my *Attention, Not Self*. Oxford, 2017, pp. 9–14, 329–31.
[19] *The Book of Disquiet*, #84. I will say more about this in the chapter, 'Building Subjects.'
[20] *Attention, Not Self*, pp. 96–101.

object but the perception of Reality itself, so to speak.'[21] More neutrally, the Zen idea of *satori* is the notion that the very subject–object structure of the field of phenomenal awareness can and must be overcome. To say that is, in effect, to reject the positional conception of self altogether in favour of something much more like Weil's uncentred mind. Buddhist 'no self', on this understanding, means centrelessness, an idea the origins of which may be traced to Nāgārjuna and the Madhyamaka school, as its influence spread throughout East Asia.

What defines Caeiro, though, is the idea that concepts are an impediment to seeing things as they are. The Buddhist philosophers who agree with this are the members of yet a third Buddhist school, the Yogācāra school, as founded by Dignāga in the fifth century CE. Dignāga's slogan is 'one sees the blue, not "it is blue"'.[22] He argues that nonconceptual perceptual experience of the particularity of the given is the only true way of knowing reality, and that concepts superimpose an erroneous structure of generality. According to his followers, the basic error is one of reification: concept-laden thought presents what are in fact merely conditioned appearances as if existing independently, as part of the real.[23] What would it be like to see the world as a Yogācāra Buddhist says we should? Or, as Dan Lusthaus puts it, 'How does the world look through enlightened eyes? How, if at all, does perception for enlightened beings differ from the way non-enlightened beings perceive?' Lusthaus has unearthed a surprisingly rare Buddhist discussion of this seemingly fundamental question, in a text written by one of Dignāga's

---

[21] Zenith, Richard. 'Alberto Caeiro as Zen heteronym'. *Portuguese Literary and Cultural Studies* 3 (1999), pp. 101–9, at p. 106. Paulo Borges highlights many differences between Caeiro and Zen in his essay 'As coisas são coisas?', *Pessoa Plural* 9 (2006), pp. 107–27. But see also Cardiello, Antonio. 'Abysmo y nada absoluto: confluencias budistas en el pensamiento de Fernando Pessoa e Nishida Kataro'. In López, Pablo Javier Pérez, and Quindós, Fernando Calderón, eds., *El Pensar Poético de Fernando Pessoa*. Editorial Manuscritos, 2010, pp. 83–170.

[22] Hattori Masaaki (trans.). *Dignāga on Perception*. Harvard, 1966, p. 26.

[23] Tillemans, Tom. 'What would it be like to be selfless? Hināyānist versions, Māhāyānist versions, and Derek Parfit'. *Asiatische Studien* 50 (1996), pp. 835–52, at p. 850: 'It would certainly not involve seeing the elements alone, nor, following Yogācāra at least, would it mean that the self (i.e. the person) would somehow vanish completely or that the world would remain strangely blank. It would be to see both the self and the world as pure "conditioned things" (*paratantra*), appearances in all their richness and diversity, but free from all traces of reification or hypostatization of entities.' I disagree with Tillemans, though, when he also claims that Theravāda is Humean: 'The consequences of actually having a prolonged experience of one's self being "reduced away" to elements in the way which the [Theravāda Buddhist] advocates might well be such that it would be difficult to see any advantage in leading such a life' (p. 849).

immediate followers.[24] While the experience of a normal, unenlightened thinker consists in the five sorts of sense perception along with introspective awareness and a reservoir of cognitive habits, all presented as 'mine' or 'belonging to me', an enlightened mind has transformed these into four sorts of cognition—named mirroring, equalizing, attentive, and activity-accomplishing. What these four sorts of cognition do is, respectively, to 'contain the images of all things, equally, without attachment', to regard 'all as the same' without the qualifier 'mine', to 'remain effortlessly focussed', and to 'perceive things just as they are thereby enabling one to accomplish all tasks'.[25] What it is like to be an enlightened being, to see things as they are, according to the earliest exponents of Dignāga, is to be in a mental state that is a perfect mirror, effortlessly attentive, and untarnished by a sense of mine-ness.

What we can say, then, is that as a heteronym 'Caeiro' denotes a nonconceptual manner of phenomenal resonance, and that this is just what Dignāga means by perception, or sensation (*pratyakṣa*), as a type of experience which is free from conceptual construction. Are there ways to introduce structure to a field of experience other than by superimposing a framework of concepts? Is there a nonconceptual way to structure the field? Ricardo Reis, a disciple of Caeiro, is the heteronymic embodiment of that idea. Things must be felt as they are, but also so as to fall in with a certain ideal of measure and rule, which Reis seeks in the classical ideal of the pagan Hellenistic schools. His way of experiencing is subject to rule and his poetic style is formal. For Caeiro's disciple Álvaro de Campos, on the other hand, the 'as they are' in 'things must be felt as they are' is superfluous. His extreme sensationism is a creed which affirms, not sensation of things as they are, but as how they are felt. Campos worships the intensity of feeling, the richness and diversity of phenomenal quality.

So the two disciples of the master Caeiro stand for two directions of movement, a strengthening and a weakening of Caeiro's sensationalism respectively, one which seeks sources of order greater than the world itself affords, and finds them in pre-established rules, the other abandoning even the world's own order in favour of diversity of phenomenal character alone. If Caeiro represents an unqualified commitment to the claim that the unity

[24] Lusthaus, Dan. 'A pre-Dharmakīrti discussion of Dignāga preserved in Chinese translation: the *Buddhabhumy-upadeśa*'. *Journal of Buddhist Studies* 6 (2009), pp. 19–81.
[25] Lusthaus, 'A pre-Dharmakīrti discussion of Dignāga preserved in Chinese translation', p. 26.

of consciousness requires that things be seen exactly as they are, Reis embodies the more Kantian thought that what this demands is for there to be a transempirical foundation, and Campos the somewhat more Humean idea that sensation is a law unto itself, that it contains within itself the sources of the unity of consciousness. Be that as it may, the point is that a mind whose contents are entirely nonconceptual *could* certainly be organized in such a way as to have a centre-periphery structure, and an uncentred mind *could* indeed have mental items with conceptual content. The non-conceptualism of a Dignāga or a Caeiro does not entail the centrelessness of a Nāgārjuna or a Weil. And centrelessness, whether with concepts or without, does not entail the disintegration of the mind into disorder.

Richard Zenith formulates Pessoa's relationship with Buddhism in terms of a dilemma:

> Buddhism went so far as to deny the existence within man not only of a relative ego but even of the absolute ego or true Self known as the *ātman*, and Pessoa's heteronymic program *might* be seen as a similar denial, a recognition that there is no permanent Self, that man is a conjunction of various elements in continual flux. *Or* is it that Pessoa, thoroughly steeped in Western culture and Western ways, wanted to pluralize his self so as to augment his ego, to make his person even more imposing, more illustrious, more influential?[26]

I would argue that there is no genuine dilemma here. We can understand both sides of Pessoa as long as we have the positional conception of self available to us. The first half of Zenith's dilemma can then be reformulated as the claim that occupancy of the central position is only contingent, an awareness of the fugitivity of self; and that it may go unoccupied altogether. The second half of the dilemma is the claim that the central position can also, nevertheless, be filled by a multiplicity of occupants, certainly one after another and perhaps even simultaneously. As long as we have the positional conception of self before us, we can makes sense of both horns of the apparent dilemma.

The radical possibility of uncentred, yet non-dysfunctional, minds is not one Pessoa admits. As we have seen, some Buddhists do say, with Simone Weil, that it is possible so to restructure one's mind as to make it centreless

---

[26] Zenith, 'Alberto Caeiro as Zen heteronym', p. 107.

and therefore, in Pessoa's sense and in theirs, selfless. Yet, in a handwritten note in his copy of George Mead's *Quests Old and New*, he writes that:

> There is no such thing as consciousness; that is, there is no such thing as consciousness itself. There are only the conscious. Only when consciousness obeys the law of plurality which is the 1st Law of Reality, then C[onscious]ness ceases to exist as consciousness, it comes to exist as Reality, it comes into being, *tout court*. There is no meaning of Consciousness, but only of the conscious I, only of the sensual error, only of the I itself.[27]

Were we to take this note to be definitive of his view, it would position Pessoa as someone who rejects the very possibility of a selfless mind. I suspect this is, indeed, his view, that the lack of centredness in a structure of conscious experience is a dysfunction, not an achievement. I have argued that such a view is compatible with the claim that Caeiro is a Buddhist heteronym, because he is, more specifically, a Yogācāra heteronym, and a mind whose landscape is populated only by unconceptualized sensations can still be a centred mind and so can still sustain a subject position, whether occupied or not. Caeiro cannot be a Zen heteronym because the Zen mind is not a heteronymic one, for heteronymic minds are centred minds. I'll go on next to consider a possibility inverse to the one discussed in this chapter, namely the possibility that a mind can be centred even if it has no sensations at all.

---

[27] Translation from Cardiello, Antonio, and Gori, Pietro. 'Nietzsche's and Pessoa's psychological fictionalism'. *Pessoa Plural* 10 (2016), pp. 578–605, at p. 594.

16

Centres without Sensibility

A fundamental claim in Pessoa's philosophy is that selves are grounded in fields of experience. 'The locus of sensations known as my soul....'[1] 'Day after day, in my ignoble and profound soul, I register the impressions that form the external substance of my self-awareness.'[2] The positional conception of self is the conception of being the one at the centre of a landscape of sensations. What, though, if there are no sensations? Is the positional conception, and the sort of 'I'-thoughts it sustains, still available in cases of total sensory deprivation? Can I think of myself as the one at the centre when there is no field of sensory experience for me to locate myself as at the centre of?

This very possibility, which seems at first sight to be wholly unavailable to Pessoa, is exactly what is countenanced by the eleventh-century Central Asian philosopher Avicenna.[3] Avicenna says that one can imagine a human being who is created out of nothing flying through the air but having no sensory perceptions:

So we say: one of us must imagine himself so that he is created all at once and perfect but his sight is veiled from seeing anything external, that he is created floating in the air or in a void so that the resistance of the air does not hit him—a hit he would have to sense—and that his limbs are separated from each other so that they do not meet or touch each other. He must then consider whether he affirms the existence of his self (*dhāt*). He will not hesitate in affirming that his self exists, but he will not thereby affirm any of his limbs, any of his intestines, the heart or the brain, or any

---

[1] *The Book of Disquiet*, #219.   [2] *The Book of Disquiet*, #341.
[3] Pessoa's library contains several books from the Persian. His copy of the *Rubaiyat*, in the translation of E. Fitzgerald, is richly annotated, and he refers to and praises Fitzgerald's notes in *The Book of Disquiet* (## 446–8). He possessed T. H. Weir's *Omar Khayam the Poet*, which includes in an appendix a translation of Avicenna's poem on the soul. He also owned H. W. Clarke's translation of Nizāmi's *Sikandar Nāma* and E. Browne's *Poems from Persian*. There does not, however, appear to be a summary of Avicenna's 'flying man' in any of the books in his library.

Virtual Subjects, Fugitive Selves: Fernando Pessoa and his Philosophy. Jonardon Ganeri, Oxford University Press (2021). © Jonardon Ganeri.
DOI: 10.1093/oso/9780198864684.001.0001

external thing. Rather, he will affirm his self without affirming for it length, breadth or depth.[4]

This man is able to grasp that he exists without grasping that he has a body, and so, it seems, is capable of a sort of self-awareness that is not grounded in sensation. Indeed, Avicenna is elsewhere clear that his view is that 'self-awareness is innate to the self, it is the self's very existence; so nothing external is needed by means of which to apprehend the self—rather, the self is that which apprehends itself.'[5]

Avicenna's thought experiment exemplifies the sort of enactive imagination for which Pessoa reserves the term of art 'dreaming'. There would appear to exist, at least as an experiential possibility, the option of imagining a scenario in which one exists and is aware of oneself but there is no landscape of sensation. Avicenna has stipulated that the imagined scenario is one in which the flying man has no visual or kinaesthetic sensations, and so his body can figure neither as one which is perceptually present before him (as when I look down and see my hands and feet positioned before me in a certain way), nor as a body image which is kinaesthetically felt, nor as one whose movements are experienced as willed. These are precisely the three dimensions of embodied centrality: 'The human being (body) that is "me" ("mine") is the one that is perceptually present in a unique way (perceptual centrality); is the one that is the locus of feeling (centrality of feeling); and is the one whose movements figure as willed (volitional centrality).'[6]

It may seem that the positional conception of self is therefore unavailable to the flying man, and if he is indeed capable of some form of self-awareness, this self-awareness could not be positional in nature. Is it then purely reflexive, a contentless mode of self-presentation? Yet I have argued against purely reflexive accounts of self-awareness, and it isn't Avicenna's account either. Jari Kaukua, in a careful study of all the texts, concludes that Avicennan 'self-awareness simply designates the fact that, regardless of what contents of experience I am aware of, they will always be given to me in a

---

[4] *On the Soul, Healing (Al-Shifā)* 15.17–16.17. Translation: Kaukua, Jari. *Self-Awareness in Islamic Philosophy: Avicenna and Beyond.* Cambridge, 2015, p. 35. Some scholars argue that the word *dhāt* in this passage refers to essence rather than self: Adamson, Peter, and Benevich, Fedor. 'The thought experimental method: Avicenna's flying man argument', *Journal of the American Philosophical Association* 4 (2018), pp. 147–64.
[5] *Ta'līqāt*, 160–1. Translation: Kaukua, *Self-Awareness*, p. 53.
[6] Valberg, *Dream, Death, and the Self*, p. 271.

first-personal perspective as so many aspects of my experience,[7] that 'Avicenna's concept of self-awareness purports to grasp nothing more than the fact that all my experience is qualified as *mine*, that no matter what I apprehend I will apprehend as an *I*, and that every act of mine is performed by me.'[8] And indeed Avicenna does seem to have a positional conception of self in mind when he claims that one is self-aware in the relevant sense even when one is asleep. Having affirmed, in another formulation of the flying man, that 'even in the case of a sleeper in his sleep or a drunk person in his drunkenness, his self will not escape his self,'[9] Avicenna also says that 'the sleeper operates on his imaginations just as he operates on the things he senses when awake, and he often operates on intellectual and cogitative things just as when awake. In the state of his operation on that he is aware that he is that operator just as he is at the state of being awake....'[10] While asleep, Avicenna says, there is volitional centrality: one is aware of oneself as the one who acts, acts at least on purely intellectual and cogitative matters and perhaps also on the sensible content of one's dreams. In this passage, therefore, Avicenna clearly relates the sort of self-awareness that the flying man thought experiment brings into view with the positional conception of self.

I will claim that there *is* a phenomenological field, and so a type of centrality, available even to the flying man. Perceptual, kinaesthetic, and embodied volitional centrality is denied to the flying man or a person in a sensory deprivation tank, but could not such a person still have feelings of a type that do not depend for their existence on perceptual experience or kinaesthetic awareness? There could be, for instance, feelings like elation, which occur independently of bodily sensation. Valberg suggests, more enigmatically, that even in a state of total sensory deprivation there would be a psychological field, a field of felt sensory emptiness: 'We can imagine our experience filled with darkness and silence, having no tactual or bodily feeling whatever. But we have not thereby imagined the complete absence of presence. There would still be *this* darkness, *this* silence—a sensory emptiness that would itself be present.'[11] I wonder if this is what Pessoa has in mind when he writes, 'Sometimes the best way to see an object is to delete it, because it subsists in a way I can't quite explain, consisting in the

---

[7] Kaukua, *Self-Awareness*, p. 71.   [8] Kaukua, *Self-Awareness*, p. 75.
[9] *Ishārat* 3, 119. Translation: Kaukua, *Self-Awareness*, p. 80.
[10] *Mubāḥathāt* 380, 210. Translation: Kaukua, *Self-Awareness*, p. 82.
[11] Valberg, *Dream, Death, and the Self*, p. 240.

substance of its negation and deletion.'[12] Whatever the specific details, the general form of the response is that there is a type of psychological centrality, a centrality of purely psychological phenomena.

Nothing, though, prevents us from simply embellishing the thought experiment to rule out this solution. Although Avicenna didn't himself say this, let us stipulate that the flying man has no purely psychic feelings either, no feeling of elation or anything else of that sort. Still, even now, it is built into the description of the imagined scenario that the flying man has thoughts of a certain sort, for he is said to 'consider whether he affirms the existence of his self', and considering is a sort of thinking. If thoughts like this are available to him, then there could indeed be a fourth field, a field of cognitive phenomenology. Avicenna himself seems to suggest something of the sort with his reference to certain 'cogitative intellectual matters', available to be acted on as much in dreaming as while awake, and presumably available to the flying man even as he affirms the existence of his self. As Kaukua puts it on behalf of Avicenna, 'if self-awareness amounts to nothing but the first-personal perspective to whatever is in one's mind, then the presence of *any mental content* will indeed be enough.'[13]

To try to imagine a scenario in which there is no landscape of sensation at all, no arena of presence and action, no experiential horizon, is not to try to imagine anything at all. As Valberg puts it,

> A total absence of presence is not like being immersed in a sensory deprivation tank...It would not be like darkness or silence. It would not be like anything. We cannot imagine it—not because it is somehow too difficult to imagine, but because there is nothing to imagine. Sensory emptiness is a limiting case of presence, an imaginable nothingness. The nothingness that is the total absence of presence is an absolute blank, an unimaginable nothingness.[14]

Again, '[T]he impossibility of imagining there being nothing present from within my horizon...is an experiential impossibility. In the case of the empty horizon, there is NOTHING—hence nothing to imagine (hence no horizon).'[15] In Pessoan terms, there is no act of dreaming that could

---

[12] 'Milky way', *The Book of Disquiet*, p. 434.
[13] Kaukua, *Self-Awareness*, p. 81; my italics.
[14] Valberg, *Dream, Death, and the Self*, p. 96.
[15] Valberg, *Dream, Death, and the Self*, p. 240.

simulate a field of total phenomenal absence because there is then nothing to simulate. If, instead of imagining oneself as the flying man, with his phenomenology at least of cogitation (what it is like to think that 2 + 2 = 4, and so on), I instead try to imagine myself as in a state of total phenomenal absence, then I must not imagine myself as having any sort of self-awareness at all, and indeed there is really nothing at all to imagine.

The claim is that a positional conception of self can be grounded in the centrality of a purely cognitive phenomenology. I am the one at the centre of all this, where what 'this' picks out is a landscape populated only by feelings of cognition, how it *feels to think* about things. A cognitive phenomenology is the distinctive phenomenology, not of experiences in the five sensory modalities including bodily sensations, nor of emotions and moods, but of consciously thinking, deliberating, puzzling, speculating, and considering. It has until recently been something of the orthodoxy in philosophy of mind to deny that there is any such thing as cognitive phenomenology: sensory, bodily, and affective phenomenology are the only phenomenologies there are, and conscious thoughts have no phenomenal character or 'what-it-is-likeness' at all. This orthodoxy has recently been challenged, and it has been claimed not only that thinking has a phenomenology, but that this phenomenology is 'proprietary', that is, that there is a kind of non-sensory phenomenal character irreducible to sensory, bodily, and affective phenomenology.[16] Others agree that such phenomenology exists but deny that it is proprietary, either because it is held that thought 'always and essentially involves, or is somehow 'realized in', a sensory medium of some sort, such as inner speech', or else because thought 'has an impact on the structure of the subject's sensory manifold [...for example] recognizing someone changes the phenomenal character of one's visual perception of them'.[17] If our attempt to call upon cognitive phenomenology to provide a manifold of presence in cases of extreme sensory deprivation such as that of the flying man is to succeed, then it is a proprietary phenomenology of non-sensory phenomenal character which will be required.

If a purely cognitive landscape of presence is a possibility, then so too is a virtual subject, a heteronym, whose manner of experiencing is purely cognitive. This purely cognitive heteronym is indeed just the self Descartes ought

---

[16] Pitt, David. 'The phenomenology of cognition, or, what is it like to think that *p*?' *Philosophy and Phenomenological Research* 69 (2004), pp. 1–36.

[17] Bayne, Timothy, and Montague, Michelle, eds. *Cognitive Phenomenology*. Oxford, 2011, p. 12.

to have described in the *First Meditation* when he imagines removing from the landscape of experience any sensory phenomenology, and finds that he cannot without self-contradiction remove thinking itself. Mark Johnston comments that, 'When Descartes uses first-person imaginings to argue that he is not essentially a body or to suggest that he is not essentially the human being Descartes, he is…observing that a certain mind or consciousness, or, as we now might put it, a certain arena of presence and action, which he can directly pick out, seems detachable from any body and hence from any human being.'[18] Pessoa says that he is 'a centre only because every circle has one',[19] and what we have discovered is that the Avicennan self is a sort of limit case for heteronymy. This is the self one simulates within oneself by imagining a phenomenal field populated only by items of pure thinking. There can, presumably, be different ways of feeling a thought, different manners in which what it is like to think that $2 + 2 = 4$ resonates within, and so different purely cognitive virtual subjects. Don Sandalio and the flying man are, for this reason, distinct from one another as two Cartesian souls never can be.

The threat posed by thought experiments involving sensory deprivation to Pessoa's philosophy of self is real. He could simply deny that the flying man is self-aware; but if he agrees with Avicenna's intuition, then the only alternative is to identify a landscape of purely cognitive feeling. We need to extend the reach of Pessoa's term of art 'sensation' to cover more than just perceptual, bodily, affective, and volitional phenomenal properties: it needs to include the feelings that are part of a cognitive phenomenology as well. We need, too, to reject accounts of cognitive phenomenology which deny that it can occur in the absence of perceptual and kinaesthetic experience. Pessoa did not countenance this extension, and his sensationism is restricted to the deliverances of the five senses, moods and emotions, pleasures and pains. So he had no name for the purely cognitive heteronym that is the Avicennan self.

I have discussed the possibility of landscapes with sensation but no centre, and the possibility of landscapes with centre but no sensation. The next idea I want to explore is that of heteronymic nesting, the possibility of assuming a heteronym which itself assumes a heteronym. I want to consider, if nesting is indeed a possibility, the nature of the relationship between the embedded heteronym and the simulating subject. This, again, is not a possibility Pessoa himself discusses; it represents a further extension in the application of his philosophy of self.

---

[18] Johnston, *Surviving Death*, p. 154.   [19] *The Book of Disquiet*, #262.

17

Dreams inside Dreams

Metaphysical dependencies between things crop up all the time, and are of different kinds. A shadow is metaphysically dependent on the object which casts it, a reflection on what is reflected, a quality on a substance, a whole on its parts. Although it seems to make no sense to say that a shadow can itself cast a shadow, it is not generally the case that entities which are metaphysically dependent on other entities cannot themselves serve in the role of ground. We find no difficulty in thinking of a picture of a picture, and a whole is made of parts, each of which may itself be a whole made of parts. Such nestable grounding relations form chains of dependence, which may or may not be transitive, meaning that if A grounds B and B grounds C, then A grounds C, and may or may not be well-founded, meaning that the chain begins somewhere.

Is heteronymic simulation, too, nestable? Pessoa assumes the heteronym Caeiro, writing poetry in the style of Caeiro. To my knowledge, Pessoa never, though, considers this scenario: Caeiro himself assumes a heteronym, who then speaks and writes as this embedded heteronym. Pessoa treats his heteronyms more like shadows than like pictures, foreclosing the possibility that a heteronym can cast its own heteronymic shadow. In all Pessoa's writings there is not a single case involving a heteronym of a heteronym.[1]

That is not to say that Pessoa is unfamiliar with the idea of nesting per se. He says, for instance, that 'this makes me fantasize about whether everything in the sum total of the world might not be an interconnected series of dreams and novels, like little boxes inside larger boxes that are inside yet

---

[1] John Frow is the only author I know of to have observed this fact. He takes it to show that heteronymy is not a nestable relation, writing that 'one of the ways in which the heteronyms and the orthonym are distinguished from "Fernando Pessoa himself" is that the heteronyms cannot themselves have heteronyms: there is no infinite spiral of multiplying and named selves.' Frow, John. *Character and Person.* Oxford, 2014, p. 221. Frow does not, however, offer any reason to deny that heteronymy is nestable other than that Pessoa does not consider the possibility. He also, here, conflates nesting with well-foundedness.

Virtual Subjects, Fugitive Selves: Fernando Pessoa and his Philosophy. Jonardon Ganeri,
Oxford University Press (2021). © Jonardon Ganeri.
DOI: 10.1093/oso/9780198864684.001.0001

larger ones.'[2] Dreams inside dreams, and their implications for the distinction between dream and reality, is also a strong thematic element in his play *The Mariner*, where the second watcher reports dreaming of a stranded mariner who dreams up a fictitious homeland.[3] In this dreamed-up homeland, Pessoa emphasizes, the mariner lives as a person among others, with friends, acquaintances, and a remembered past. When Pessoa writes, 'Then he travelled, with his memory, through the country he'd created',[4] the pronoun 'he' appears twice, once to refer to the mariner who is the dreaming subject, and again to refer to the subject-within-the-dream. The dream acquires such vivacity that in the end it seems to be his actual life and he is unable to remember his true homeland: 'Whereas in the life he thought he'd merely dreamed, everything was real and had existed…he couldn't even dream, couldn't even conceive, of having had any other past.'[5] The second watcher says that all is explained by another detail in the story: when a boat arrives at the island on which he had been stranded, the mariner is not there. As embedded within the context of a dream, it is the subject-within-the-dream who is real, the dreaming subject less so. Embedding, the lesson seems to be, inverts metaphysical priority.

These are, evidently, Borgesian topics, and the character of dreams inside dreams is the implied theme of Borges's story *The Circular Ruins*. Borges introduces the idea that the relation between dreaming subject and simulacrum is nested when he has the 'foreigner' who dreams a youth into being discover, in the dramatic final sentences of the story, that he is himself a simulacrum in another dreamer's dream. What the foreigner learns in this moment is that the Cartesian dream hypothesis is true: all this *is* a dream, a dream within which there is a dream in which the youth is dreamt into being.

Nested dreams, together with their implications for the reality of subjects, are more explicitly the theme of a remarkable passage in the third-century BCE Daoist classic, the *Zhuangzi*. Here is how the passage reads in Brook Ziporyn's translation:

> Once Zhuang Zhou dreamt he was a butterfly, fluttering about joyfully just as a butterfly would. He followed his whims exactly as he liked and knew nothing about Zhuang Zhou. Suddenly he awoke, and there he was, the startled Zhuang Zhou in the flesh. He did not know if Zhou had been dreaming he was a butterfly, or if a butterfly was now dreaming it was

---

[2] *The Book of Disquiet*, #285.   [3] *The Mariner*. In *Selected Prose*, pp. 20–34.
[4] *The Mariner*. In *Selected Prose*, p. 28.   [5] *The Mariner*. In *Selected Prose*, p. 29.

Zhou. Surely, Zhou and a butterfly count as two distinct identities! Such is what we call the transformation of one thing into another.[6]

A similar double scenario features in Julio Cortázar's story 'The night face up'. A man in a hospital ward falls asleep and dreams he is a Moteca, fleeing from the Aztecs. He awakens, but on falling asleep again has the same dream, and repeatedly so. At long last it occurs to him that he really is a Moteca, dreaming of being a contemporary man in a hospital bed.[7] The *Zhuangzi* version has an intriguingly complex structure. There is a framing dream exhibiting self-alienation, Zhou's dream being such that, within the dream, the one at the centre of the landscape of presence is a butterfly. There is then an 'emergence' from the dream, a 'waking' with Zhou now present in the flesh. Immediately, however, two alternative explanations of this 'emergence' are countenanced. One is the commonplace idea that Zhou, having fallen asleep, now awakens and recalls the dream he just had. The other, more complicated, suggestion, is that the butterfly falls asleep and has its own self-alienated dream, within which the one at the centre of the landscape of presence is Zhou. Some interpreters prefer to read the second alternative as simply that it was a butterfly all along, dreaming it was Zhou. Yet in this reading there is still nesting, because the butterfly dreams it is Zhou who dreams he is a butterfly. Either way, then, the story is about a nested dream.

With the apparatus of Pessoa's philosophy of self to hand, we can understand this complicated story in a fresh light. The framing dream represents a by-now familiar case. It is just the same as Valberg's example of dreaming that he is X. This is not a case of Zhou dreaming that he, Zhou the human being, inhabits the body of a butterfly; rather, in Zhou's dream, it is the butterfly which is the one at the centre of a butterflyish field of consciousness. We might retell this stage of the parable thus: 'Once Pessoa imagined he was a fly, fluttering about joyfully just as a fly would. He followed his whims exactly as he liked and knew nothing about Pessoa.' That is almost exactly the same as Pessoa's actual remark: 'I really felt like a fly when I imagined I felt like one. And I felt I had a flyish soul, slept flyishly and was flyishly withdrawn.'[8] The personal pronoun is, therefore, used positionally.

---

[6] *Zhuangzi: The Essential Writings*, translated by Brook Ziporyn. Hackett, 2009, p. 21.

[7] Cortázar, Julio. *La noche boca arriba*. In *The End of the Game, and Other Stories*, translated by Paul Blackburn. Pantheon, 1963.

[8] *The Book of Disquiet*, #334.

Classical Chinese indeed has two words for 'I', *wu* and *wo*. In an earlier passage of the *Zhuangzi* Ziqi says, 'Now I (*wu*) have lost myself (*wo*)'.[9] Commentators generally associate *wu* with 'an idea of naked subjectivity of experience' or a 'thin subject of experience',[10] and *wo* with the fleshed-out human being. Yet, exactly as with Pessoa's statement, 'I am no longer I', what we should say is that the first person is used in two distinct ways: the first use of 'I' is a positional use and the second use is a simple indexical use. Classical Chinese, unlike English, marks the positional use of the first person lexically. It is no longer the human being Ziqi who figures as the one at the centre of the field of consciousness: the fugitive self has lost track of the human being with whom it has long, but still only contingently, been one. Likewise here: Zhou has 'lost himself' in the sense that, within the dream, he is a butterfly and no longer a human being.

Two distinct scenarios are now envisaged, each of which might constitute what it is to 'emerge' from the dream. One is that Zhou awakens and recalls that, in the dream, he was the butterfly. Valberg and Johnston have both provided accounts of what it is to emerge from a dream in this mundane sense. For Johnston, it is a repopulating of the phenomenal field now with veridical perceptions. He writes, 'When I awake and recall that I was dreaming that I was flying, an apparently common frame grounds these "I"-uses. That apparent common frame is an arena that with my awaking has apparently come to include a host of veridical perceptions.'[11] Valberg, in the grip of the idea that the field is unique and alone, instead represents emergence from a dream as consisting in a widening of the horizon, a larger horizon that now includes the contents of the dream.[12] The alternative scenario is harder to understand. What is now envisaged is that, still in the dream, the butterfly falls asleep and dreams that it is Zhuang Zhou. This second, embedded dream is also self-alienated, but now it is the butterfly who is the dreaming subject, and it is Zhou who is, in the nested dream, the subject-within-the-dream, the one at the centre of the landscape of dreamt sensations.

Were all this to be put in terms of heteronymic simulation, Pessoan 'dreaming' rather than actual dreaming, it would be an illustration of nested heteronyms and of a rather particular sort. It would be as if Pessoa assumes

---

[9] *Zhuangzi: The Essential Writings*, p. 12.
[10] Hung, Jenny. 'The theory of the self in the *Zhuangzi*: A Strawsonian interpretation'. *Philosophy East and West* 69 (2019), pp. 376–94.
[11] Johnston, *Surviving Death*, p. 188.   [12] Valberg, *Dream, Death, and the Self*, p. 121.

the heteronym Caeiro, who then assumes a heteronym. The heteronym Caeiro assumes, however, is Fernando Pessoa himself! In his actual writings Pessoa does not consider the possibility of heteronymic nesting, and even less does he consider the possibility the *Zhuangzi* explores, that of *circular* heteronymic nesting. The nearest he comes is in recounting how he composed an 'early Campos' poem:

> I suggested to Sá-Carneiro that I write an 'old' poem of Álvaro de Campos's—a poem such as Álvaro de Campos would have written before meeting Caeiro and falling under his influence. That's how I came to write *Opiary*, in which I tried to incorporate all the latent tendencies of Álvaro de Campos that would eventually be revealed but that still showed no hint of contact with his master Caeiro. Of all the poems I've written, this was the one that gave me the most trouble, because of the twofold depersonalization it required.[13]

Heteronymic nesting, were it even to be possible, would involve a similar sort of twofold simulation. It would require Pessoa, as Campos, to assume another heteronym, Caeiro say. The case we are now considering would complicate matters still further, for the heteronym Campos would assume would be Pessoa.

When this hypothetical 'Pessoa' writes poetry, it is Pessoa-as-Campos-as-Pessoa who is writing, and the puzzle is to know how this poet stands in relation to Pessoa. 'Surely,' the *Zhuangzi* says, 'Zhou and a butterfly count as two distinct identities! Such is what we call the transformation of one thing into another.' A 'transformation' of one thing into another, in the context of self-alienated dreaming, is a switch in the occupancy of the subject position. Valberg 'transforms' himself into X, in this sense, when he dreams he is X. When the butterfly 'transforms' itself into Zhou, because it has a dream in which Zhou is the one at the centre, are we to suppose that this embedded 'Zhou', a subject within an embedded dream, is the same as the framing dream's dreaming subject? That is the question about identity and equivalence the story is seeking to explore.

I suggest that we answer this question by making use of a concept I have already introduced, that of an orthonym. The correct thing to say is that the embedded 'Zhou' is an orthonym of the dreaming Zhou. This embedded

---

[13] Letter to Adolfo Casais Monteiro, 13 January 1935, *Selected Prose*, p. 257.

Zhou is the double of the dreaming Zhou and is his shadow self. Each, it is affirmed, is as real as the other, but they are not identical. Recall Giorgio Agamben's description of the orthonymic mechanism: 'A new poetic consciousness, something like a genuine *ēthos* of poetry, begins once Fernando Pessoa, having survived his own depersonalization, returns to a self who both is and is no longer the first subject.' Zhou, surviving a transformation first into a butterfly and then back into himself, returns as a self who 'both is and is no longer' the original, dreaming, Zhou.

What the parable teaches us, then, is that simulating subjects are no more real than simulated subjects, and no less so. Or, as Pessoa himself puts the matter, 'The author of these books cannot affirm that all these different and well-defined personalities who have incorporeally passed through his soul don't exist, for he does not know what it means to exist, nor whether Hamlet or Shakespeare is more real, or truly real.'[14] In extending Pessoa's discussion with the introduction of a double and circular application of dream embedding, the brilliance of the parable of the butterfly in the *Zhuangzi* is that it constructs a device to answer that question: Hamlet (qua heteronym of Shakespeare, not merely a character in one of his plays) and Shakespeare are equivalently real.

---

[14] [Aspects], in *Selected Prose*, p. 2.

18

Building Subjects

Let us call any system capable of generating a conscious self an Ego Machine.... Under what conditions would we be justified in assuming that a given postbiotic system has conscious experience? Or that it also possesses a conscious self and a genuine consciously experienced first-person perspective? What turns an information-processing system into a subject of experience? We can nicely sum up these questions by asking a simpler and more provocative one: What would it take to build an artificial Ego Machine?[1]

These are the words of the philosopher Thomas Metzinger, who is known for denying, on neuroscientific grounds, that there is a self. Every attempt to achieve a physicalist reduction of the mind has failed, and failed in large part because of increasingly more sophisticated understanding of what makes conscious experience such a unique and distinctive part of the natural world. It is now customary to draw a distinction between the phenomenal quality of experience, what it is like to undergo an experience of some sort, and the subjective character of experience, the fact that experience is for a subject, the for-me-ness in the phrase 'what it is like for me to savour the mango's flesh.' The irreducibility of the phenomenal quality of phenomenal experience has been called the 'hard problem' about consciousness: physical properties do not seem to be of remotely the right sort to ground phenomenal qualities.

Panpsychism proposes to finesse the problem by claiming that consciousness already belongs within fundamental reality, claiming that even particulate matter instantiates micro-psychological properties. Panpsychists do not, nowadays, claim that *everything* exhibits psychological features, but, more modestly, that psychological features are among the most fundamental features there are. As David Chalmers has put it,

---

[1] Metzinger, Thomas. *The Ego Tunnel: The Science of the Mind and the Myth of the Self.* Basic Books, 2009, pp. 187, 190.

Virtual Subjects, Fugitive Selves: Fernando Pessoa and his Philosophy. Jonardon Ganeri, Oxford University Press (2021). © Jonardon Ganeri. DOI: 10.1093/oso/9780198864684.001.0001

Panpsychism, taken literally, is the doctrine that everything has a mind. In practice, people who call themselves panpsychists are not committed to as strong a doctrine. They are not committed to the thesis that the number two has a mind, or that the Eiffel Tower has a mind, or that the city of Canberra has a mind, even if they believe in the existence of numbers, towers, and cities. Instead, we can understand panpsychism as the thesis that some fundamental physical entities have mental states.[2]

It is not hard to see, however, that panpsychism has it's own 'hard problem'. Whatever it is that it's like to savour the taste of a mango, this sophisticated mental property is going to be quite unlike any micro-psychological property exhibited by particulate matter. If panpsychism is true, it seems that it must be possible to build the *macro*-psychological features of creatures like us from those *micro*-psychological features, and yet these two sorts of features are radically disalike. That has been called the 'combination problem' for panpsychism.

There is an even harder problem, though, which is to understand how panpsychism can account for the subjective character of experience. Are we to suppose that each of us is literally built out of micro-subjects? But atoms are not subjects: being a subject requires having a first-personal perspective, and that is a sophisticated psychological achievement, one which micro-particulate matter does not exhibit. Pessoa, indeed, in an early philosophical essay, anticipates two versions of panpsychism. He explicitly considers the idea that human subjects are composed from micro-subjects, which he calls 'monads': 'The human soul may be composed, as we may say, by degrees. Suppose the mind is formed of one kind of monads, or spiritual atoms; make out that a small grouping of these produces the lower faculties, and so on, progressively, the intellect being the highest aggregation.'[3] That the 'spiritual atoms' are micro-subjects is clear because this is composition by degree only; the elements from which subjects are composed are the same in kind as subjects themselves. Pessoa rejects this solution to the

---

[2] Chalmers, David. 'Panpsychism and panprotopsychism'. In Brüntrup, Godehard, and Jaskola, Ludwig, eds., *Panpsychism: Contemporary Perspectives*. Oxford, 2016, pp. 19–48, at. p. 19.

[3] 'Essay on Free Will', in *Philosophical Essays: A Critical Edition*, edited and translated by Nuno Ribeiro. Contra Mundum Press, 2012, pp. 54–5. If by 'spiritual atoms' Pessoa has in mind something akin to Leibnizian monads, then this passage reveals that heteronyms, virtual subjects, are not themselves monads.

grounding problem for subjects: 'I do not think that any one has ever had this theory, neither shall I call it mine.'[4]

The other version of panpsychism he considers is one of composition 'both in nature and in degree; supposing, I mean to say, agglomerations of particles of different nature, rising in power, or perchance purifying itself into oneness'.[5] Perhaps, then, the way to build subjects is to start with micro-psychological elements that are not yet themselves subjects. The basic psychological elements will have phenomenal properties but no subjective character, so there is no attempt to build subjects out of micro-subjects. This variety of panpsychism proposes to build subjects out of impersonal sensations. Could this indeed be what Pessoa has in mind when he says, 'I am…an architect dedicated to building myself out of sensations'?[6] And, again, when he says, 'I am nothing—just an abstract centre of impersonal sensations, a fallen sentient mirror reflecting the world's diversity'?[7] What one must do, it would seem, is isolate the mechanisms that organize and maintain impersonal micro-psychological features in a centre-periphery structure, for whenever a system of such features has that structure the positional conception of self is available to it.

A version of this very strategy is to be seen at work in one of the principal schools of Buddhism, the Abhidhamma of Theravāda philosophers writing in Pāli, and especially in the writings of the fifth-century scholar Buddhaghosa. Pessoa was, surprisingly, well acquainted with Buddhaghosa's philosophy, even if he didn't know it under that description. That he had made a careful reading of George Mead's book *Quests Old and New* is clear from the many comments and annotations in his personal copy.[8] Chapter V of this book, 'Some Features of Buddhist Psychology', is a detailed review of Shwe Zan Aung's then recently published translation of the *Abhidhammattha-saṅgaha*, Anuruddha's tenth-century synopsis of the Theravāda philosophy of Buddhaghosa.[9] Mead quotes Aung as saying, 'I am but an interpreter of Burmese views based on the Ceylon Commentary and

---

[4] 'Essay on Free Will', p. 55. It has taken until now for someone to claim this theory as their own: Roelofs, Luke. *Combining Minds: How to Think about Composite Subjectivity.* Oxford, 2019.

[5] 'Essay on Free Will', p. 55.

[6] 'Sentimental education', in *The Book of Disquiet*, p. 455.

[7] *The Book of Disquiet*, #84.

[8] Mead, G. R. S. *Quests Old and New.* G. Bell & Sons, 1913. Pessoa's personal copy is available in the Casa Fernando Pessoa.

[9] *Compendium of Philosophy*, translated by Aung, Shwe Zan. London: Pali Text Society, 1910.

the works of Buddhaghosa,[10] and he offers his own opinion, that Buddhaghosa's 'analysis of mind as normally known must be admitted to be one of the acutest that has ever been thought out',[11] adding that 'the most elaborate study of man which the East has ever produced cannot be without interest to us in the West'.[12] He includes a careful description of Buddhaghosa's compositional theory of consciousness, at one point saying that 'finally we have the *alpha* and *omega* of an act of consciousness in the selective or co-ordinating activity of attention'.[13] He also discusses at length the Theravāda theory of no-self and personal identity.

Buddhaghosa argues that subjects are built out of the impersonal components of a mental life (*dhamma*, in Pāli), exactly as houses are built out of bricks:

> Just as when the component parts such as axles, wheels, frame poles, etc., are arranged in a certain way, there comes to be the mere term of common usage 'chariot', yet in the ultimate sense when each part is examined there is no chariot,—and just as when the component parts of a house such as wattles, etc., are placed so that they enclose a space in a certain way, there comes to be the mere term of common usage 'house', yet in the ultimate sense there is no house...so too, when there are the five aggregates (*khandha*) [as objects] of clinging, there comes to be the mere term of common usage 'a being', 'a person', yet in the ultimate sense, when each component is examined, there is no being as a basis for the assumption 'I am' or 'I'; in the ultimate sense there is only minded body.[14]

The five 'aggregates' of Abhidhamma Buddhism are the five sorts of psychological item that constitute a Buddhist landscape of presence. We may translate them as registration, affect, labelling, readying, and cognizing. Registering is an embodied process of somatosensory impact with one's physical surroundings. As well as registering the surroundings, the mind subsumes what it registers into a stereotypical scheme of classification, for example by labelling a red sensation *as* red, and it affectively appraises what is registered—as harmful, helpful, or indifferent, as worth pursuing or avoiding. The physical world thus comes to present itself as a structured

---

[10] Mead, *Quests Old and New*, p. 97.   [11] Mead, *Quests Old and New*, pp. vii–viii.
[12] Mead, *Quests Old and New*, pp. 95–6.   [13] Mead, *Quests Old and New*, p. 111.
[14] *Visuddhimagga* 593–4 [xviii.28]. Translated by Ñāṇamoli, Bhikkhu, *The Path of Purification: Visuddhimagga by Bhadantācariya Buddhaghosa*. Buddhist Publication Society, 5th edn., 1991, p. 617.

space of opportunities and dangers. Repeated exposure to such a world leads one to form dispositions of habitual response: the mind readies itself for future encounters based on memory of past ones. In this way, particular registrations acquire new dispositional propensities with respect to one other, as a particular smell might come to dispose one to particular feelings. Pessoan 'sensation' largely overlaps with this schema, although, let us note, the conceptualizing aspect introduced by labels is exactly what is bracketed by Caeiro, and the evaluative aspect of appraisal is what Campos seeks to put on hold.[15]

The Buddhist text just quoted, and many others like it, reject a metaphysical view Jonathan Schaffer has called 'priority monism', the view that the whole is a fundamental reality whose constituent parts are grounded in it.[16] A monist would say that the chariot, as a whole, is fundamental and that the existence of axles and wheels is derivative. A monist about selves will say that the existence of the self as an interconnected entity is what is fundamental, and the constituent psychological items depend for their existence on that; perhaps in the way a dent depends for its existence on a surface. Priority monism about subjects is exactly what Buddhists reject: there is no 'I' in the sense of a reality which is more fundamental than the reality of these constituent psychological items. What about when we say that it is the house to which the bricks belong, or that it is the self which experiences pleasure and pain? Buddhaghosa replies that this is just a figure of speech, a way of singling out one aspect of the complex construction:

> For just as it is simply owing to the arising of tree fruits which are *one part* of the states called a tree, that it is said that 'the tree fruits' or 'has fruited', so it is simply owing to the arising of the fruit consisting of the pleasure and pain called experience, which is *one part* of the aggregates called 'deities' and 'humans', that it is said that 'a deity or a human being experiences or feels pleasure or pain'. There is therefore no need at all for a [separate] experiencer.[17]

---

[15] Pessoa agrees with Buddhaghosa too that the experience of death is that of a breakdown in the arena. I discuss the affinities in my 'Illusions of immortality', in *Imaginations of Death and Beyond in India and Europe*, edited by Sudhir Kakar and Günter Blamberger. Delhi, 2018, pp. 35–45.

[16] Schaffer, Jonathan. 'Monism: the priority of the whole'. *Philosophical Review* 119 (2010), pp. 31–76.

[17] *Visuddhimagga* 555 [xvii.171–2]; *The Path of Purification*, p. 575.

To say this is to make the case that what 'house' and 'self' pick out are structural features of the assemblage, and not entities which exist independently of that assemblage. In the case of the assemblage which is a landscape of sensation, the structure in question is a centre-periphery structure, and what terms like 'self' or 'experiencer' pick out is the fact that within the phenomenology a subject position is defined.

How can a mind that is not yet centred come to be centred? We cannot beg the question by supposing that such a mind already harbours an agent-self that does the centring. Instead we must isolate cognitive processes that have this as their outcome. One contemporary panpsychist, Sam Coleman, rightly says that 'panpsychists must relinquish micro-subjects of experience…and should aim to construct a relational account of high-level subjectivity', adding that 'the success of the…panpsychist project frankly hangs on development of an adequate relational model of subjectivity'.[18] Buddhaghosa aims to provide a model of exactly the sort Coleman calls for.[19] Any single moment of consciousness is an interconnected dynamical system whose components are: aboutness or directedness, presence, felt evaluation, identificatory type, effortful control or intending, sustaining of cognitive boundaries, attentional placing, and attentional focusing.[20] Attention is a structuring principle in conscious experience, and it is because of attention that conscious experience has the sort of centre-periphery structure that sustains the positional conception of self. It was his appreciation of the fundamental importance given to attention in Buddhaghosa's philosophy of mind that led Mead to say, 'finally we have the *alpha* and *omega* of an act of consciousness in the selective or co-ordinating activity of attention'.[21]

As I have mentioned, there are hints of the sort of psychological constructivism that we find so elaborately worked out in panpsychist Abhidhamma in some of Pessoa's remarks. When Pessoa refers to sensations as 'impersonal' he means that they aren't micro-subjects, monads. His view is not, though, that they can exist independently of and prior to centred structures of experience, and that is why, for him, all consciousness

---

[18] Coleman, Sam. 'The real combination problem: panpsychism, micro-subjects, and emergence'. *Erkenntnis* 79 (2014), pp. 19–44, at p. 43.
[19] See my *Attention, Not Self* (Oxford, 2017) for a book-length discussion of Buddhaghosa's Theravāda philosophy of mind and its way of solving the subject constitution problem.
[20] *Visuddhimagga* 589 [xviii.8]; *The Path of Purification*, p. 611. *Attention, Not Self*, pp. 37–47.
[21] Mead, *Quests Old and New*, p. 111.

is personal. So the metaphors of 'building' and 'constructing' are not an entirely happy fit with his developed philosophical position. Indeed, within his heteronymic philosophy of self a quite different approach to the topic is available. In the pages of this book I have described in some detail one Ego Machine, one system capable of generating a conscious self: Fernando Pessoa. Any system with the capacity to create and simulate heteronyms is an Ego Machine. Evidently enough, only a self-conscious being which already is an I can be 'an other I'. The question, then, is not how to construct subjects *ex nihilo* out of impersonal sensations, but rather how, as a subject, to make oneself into another subject.

Perhaps this is the only question that can be answered, and Pessoa provides the materials for an answer in the theory of heteronymic simulation. The idea is to take one concrete subject and derive from it other subjects. Since the derivation relation is evidently heteronymy, let me call this view 'heteropsychism'. Its basic assumption is that nothing can turn a system that is not yet a subject of experience into one: simulation only works from within a first-person perspective. Heteropsychism is, therefore, a *modest* solution to the problem, where by the term 'modest' what I have in mind is a theoretical notion from philosophy of language, its use there being to refer to the idea that a theory of meaning should only try to show 'which concepts are associated with which words' and not participate in the more ambitious task of explaining what it is to have those concepts to someone who does not already possess them.[22] Likewise, a modest solution to the hard problem does not attempt to build subjects out of psychological materials that do not yet display subjective character, still less out of micro-subjects in combination; it limits itself to the task of showing, to a being who is already a subject, what it is to be another one. It is a theoretical account of how to construct a subject, but one which is available only to beings who are already subjects. Just as, although a whole jigsaw puzzle is metaphysically dependent on the individual pieces, we would have no idea how to put the pieces together in the right order unless we had a blueprint to work from, so, even if subjects are metaphysically dependent on the constituent elements in fields of experience, building a subject out of those elements is something only a subject can do.

I hesitate firmly to attribute heteropsychism to Pessoa himself, though there are hints of it in remarks such as 'I am...an architect dedicated to

---

[22] Modesty, in the sense used here, is a notion drawn from Michael Dummett's philosophy of language. Dummett, Michael. 'What is a theory of meaning (I)?' In his *The Seas of Language*, Oxford, 1993, pp. 1–33.

building myself',[23] and '[W]e are all equally derived from no one knows what; we're shadows of gestures performed by someone else, embodied effects, consequences that feel.'[24] The derivation of subjects, their construction out of unspecified materials, is an act performed by a subject. What I am willing to claim is that heteropsychism is a new solution to the problem of subject constitution, and that it is the apparatus of Pessoa's heteronymic philosophy of self which makes it available to us. It is the thesis that only subjects can build subjects out of sensations.

[23] 'Sentimental education', *The Book of Disquiet*, p. 455.
[24] *The Book of Disquiet*, #149.

19

The Cosmos and I

Could it be the case that all of us as individual human subjects stand to one another as Caeiro stands to Reis and Reis to Campos: just as they are the multiple heteronyms of one and the same subject, Fernando Pessoa, so too we are all heteronyms of one and the same subject, a single cosmic subject? There is a famous line in the *Chāndogya Upaniṣad* which might be interpreted as saying something of the sort—*tat tvam asi*: you are that, that single cosmic subject, *brahman*.[1] Perhaps this is simply another instance of a formula we have encountered time and again, the formula 'In my dream, I am X'. Can we read it as an expression of the thought that you, whoever you are, are a heteronym of *brahman*?

For the eighth-century Vedāntic philosopher Śaṅkara, whose reading of the Upaniṣads would much later establish itself in the popular imagination, the similarity is further reinforced because he provides a context of phenomenological simulation similar to dreaming and imagining, namely, *māyā*, 'cosmic illusion'. Drawing on such Upaniṣadic statements as 'One should recognize the illusion (*māyā*) as primal matter, and the illusionist (*māyin*), as the great Lord. This whole living world is thus pervaded by things that are parts of him',[2] Śaṅkara suggests that it is only within this illusion that you and I are distinct, just as it is within the context of Pessoa's simulations that Campos and Reis are distinct and within Valberg's dream that X and JV are distinct. Mark Johnston objects to something he calls 'Kantian Vedāntism', the doctrine that 'behind each individual consciousness there lies [*brahman*], a single noumenal self, the one who is dreaming the dream of waking life, including the dream of the separate selves that appear to inhabit waking life', finding problematic the 'highly conjectural metaphysics, not a claim about some emergent entity, which are ten-a-penny and easily constructed from any principle of unity, but instead a

---

[1] *Chāndogya Upaniṣad* 6.8.7. In *The Early Upaniṣads*, translated by Patrick Olivelle. Oxford, 1998, p. 253.
[2] *Śvetāśvatara Upaniṣad* 4.1.10. In *The Early Upaniṣads*, p. 425.

Virtual Subjects, Fugitive Selves: Fernando Pessoa and his Philosophy. Jonardon Ganeri,
Oxford University Press (2021). © Jonardon Ganeri.
DOI: 10.1093/oso/9780198864684.001.0001

claim about what is fundamentally real, namely a single noumenal Self *behind* the illusory separate selves that embroil us in our everyday egoism.[3] Yet, first, the idea that the cosmos is both conscious and the most fundamental reality has gained considerable traction in recent philosophy of mind, where it goes by the name 'cosmopsychism'.[4] And, second, within a Pessoan philosophy of self it is perfectly straightforward to say in general that one self is 'behind' another. The 'behind' relation is simply one of heteronymic simulation. The claim can be reformulated as being that *brahman* simulates each individual self, which as such are its heteronyms. As Pessoa is to his coterie of heteronyms, so *brahman* is to the mass of human selves.[5] Perhaps, indeed, there is the premonition of just such a claim in another important Upaniṣadic passage, 'And it thought to itself: "Let me become many."'[6] If there is something objectionable about the formulation of the doctrine in Śaṅkara, it is rather the idealist implication that as parts of an illusion individual selves are not real.

What we discovered in our earlier analysis of the positional use of 'I' is that such statements, although apparently having the logical form of an identity, are in actuality predications, with the predicate '...is the one at the centre of this field of consciousness' ascribed to whomsoever it is that is being said to occupy the subject position. 'In my dream, I am X' states that the predicate '...is the one at the centre of this field of dream-experience' is true of X. Applying this point to the logic of '*tat tvam asi*' would lead us to say that it is not literally an identity statement but rather that what it states is that each of us has the property of being the one who is at the centre of this, *brahmanic* field of consciousness. And indeed there are Upaniṣadic passages which permit a positional interpretation, such as this, again from the *Chāndogya Upaniṣad*: 'All alone, it will remain in the middle.'[7] An argument to this effect is most explicitly provided by the late-tenth-century Śaiva thinker Abhinavagupta. He says that 'whatever manifests itself has the shape

---

[3] Johnston, *Surviving Death*, p. 348.

[4] Shani, Itay. 'Cosmopsychism: A holistic approach to the metaphysics of consciousness.' *Philosophical Papers* 44 (2015), pp. 389–437; Nagasawa, Yujin, and Wager, Khai. 'Panpsychism and priority cosmopsychism'. In Brüntrup, Godehard, and Jaskola, Ludwig, eds., *Panpsychism: Contemporary Perspectives*. Oxford, 2016, pp. 113–29; Goff, Philip. *Consciousness and Fundamental Reality*. Oxford, 2017.

[5] At a more mundane level, with its idea that the gods have multiple *avatāras*, and even multiple heads, popular Hinduism affords much that is Pessoan in flavour. On polytheism and Pessoa's neopaganism, see Dix, Steffen. 'The plurality of gods and man, or "The aesthetic attitude in all its pagan splendor" in Fernando Pessoa.' *The Pluralist* 5 (2010), pp. 73–93.

[6] *Chāndogya Upaniṣad* 6.2.3. In *The Early Upaniṣads*, p. 247.

[7] *Chāndogya Upaniṣad* 3.11.1. In *The Early Upaniṣads*, p. 205.

of an "I". So even the awareness of another is oneself, the otherness is only of the adjuncts such as bodies... Thus, at the level of ultimate truth, all thinkers about the world are only one thinker, and it alone exists.'[8]

Let me call the view that individual human subjects are heteronyms of a single cosmic self 'heteronymic cosmopsychism'. Heteronymic cosmopsychism is different from a comparatively more common variety of cosmopsychism, one according to which the grounding relation between the single cosmic self and the multiplicity of individual selves is mereological, not heteronymic. This so-called 'priority cosmopsychism' claims to ground individual selves by subsuming them in the cosmic self by way of a decomposition relation.[9] Yet the idea that the grounding relation is mereological is a source of several serious difficulties. Itay Shani and Joachim Keppler observe, for instance, that

> part of what makes the subject constitution problem so intractable is that it has been shown to repeatedly involve serious conceptual aporia... [M]ost, if not all, of these conceptual tangles appear to be related to the assumption that one perspectival subject is literally composed of, or fractured from, another. In the idiom of cosmopsychism, the assumption is that the cosmos itself is a universal mind and that all lesser minds partake in it like coloured tiles cut from a jigsaw puzzle's cardboard model— each carrying about itself a small piece of the grand picture.[10]

The two basic problems with priority cosmopsychism are, first, that conscious subjects do not decompose any more than they compose, and, second, that the cosmic self cannot have a perspective of its own. For what is the perspective of the cosmic subject? Does the idea that the cosmos has a perspective

---

[8] Abhinavagupta, *Īśvara-pratyabhijñā-vivṛti-vimarśinī* under 1.1.4. Translation: Chakrabarti, Arindam. 'Arguing from synthesis to self: Utpaladeva and Abhinavagupta respond to Buddhist no-self'. In Irina Kuznetsova, Jonardon Ganeri, and Chakravarthi Ram-Prasad, eds. *Hindu and Buddhist Ideas in Dialogue: Self and No-Self*. Routledge, 2012, pp. 199–216, at p. 213. Rehan Visser has associated Pessoa with the poetician of whom Abhinavagupta was a disciple, Ānandavardhana. Visser, Rehan. 'Fernando Pessoa's art of living: ironic multiplicities, multiple ironies'. *Philosophical Forum* 50 (2019), pp. 435–545, at p. 452, n. 110.

[9] Goff, Philip. *Consciousness and Fundamental Reality*. Oxford, 2017. A much earlier source for the view is *Bhagavad-gītā* 15.7, where Kṛṣṇa describes individual selves as his own parts: 'Just a fragment of me in the realm of the living is the permanent individual self'. Patton, Laurie, trans. *The Bhagavad Gītā*. Penguin Classics, 2008, p. 238.

[10] Shani, Itay, and Keppler, Joachim. 'Beyond combination: How cosmic consciousness grounds ordinary experience'. *Journal of the American Philosophical Association* (2018), pp. 390–410, at p. 405.

THE COSMOS AND I   141

even make sense, given that a perspective is a partial view from a particular location?[11] Perspectival subjects are 'localized centers of consciousness; they experience reality in a constrained and selective manner, through specific channels, portals, and filters (as it were); finally, although their field of experience is unified, it is structured and dually framed: presenting objects as given to an underlying apprehending recipient.'[12] It does not seem possible to say that the cosmos is a 'perspectival subject' in this sense, because it does not have a specific location and its experience is not narrowly framed.

What heteronymic cosmopsychism claims, in contrast, is that there are multiple heteronyms of the fundamental cosmic self. The grounding relation is heteronymic, not decompositional, and the problems which are so fatal to priority cosmopsychism simply do not arise. In particular, the claim that the positional conception of self is available to a cosmic self is distinct from the claim that the cosmic self has a spatio-temporal perspective: being the one at the centre of a landscape of sensation need not be partial in the way having a perspective essentially is. That is because in addition to the three perspectival kinds of embodied centrality identified by Valberg—perceptual centrality, centrality of feeling, and volitional centrality[13]—there are also non-perspectival sources of centrality, such as the centrality exhibited by the purely cognitive phenomenology of an Avicennan mind and the centrality exhibited by a virtual subject constituted by a style of feeling that is purely literary. Perspective is, indeed, 'a partial view from a particular location', whereas centrality is fundamentally a matter of experience having an addressee, and this need be neither partial nor from a particular spatio-temporal location. That phenomenal centrality and perspective are distinct is also a lesson one might draw from our earlier discussions of the painting Las Meninas and the story of the philosopher Sulabhā, if one can say that in such cases there are two phenomenal centres occupying one and the same perspectival point of view (Sulabhā, recall, places herself in the soul of Janaka and begins an internal dialogue with him).

Heteronymic cosmopsychism begins with the idea that there is a cosmic self, and that this single cosmic self is the fundamental metaphysical ground of individual selves, the grounding relation being one of heteronymic simulation. Although I have drawn on the notion of heteronymy to present this

---

[11] Albahari, Miri. 'Beyond cosmopsychism and the great I am: how the world might be grounded in universal "Advaitic" consciousness'. In William Seager, ed. *The Routledge Handbook of Panpsychism*. Routledge, 2020, pp. 119–130.
[12] Shani and Keppler, 'Beyond combination', p. 404.
[13] Valberg, *Dream, Death, and the Self*, p. 271.

solution to the grounding problem for subjects, I do not believe that the Pessoa of the heteronymic poems, or indeed the author of the semi-heteronymic *Book of Disquiet*, is a cosmopsychist.[14] The cosmopsychist Pessoa is the Pessoa who was an avid student of neopaganism and the esoteric. My principal textual evidence for this claim is a single remarkable passage:

> It is difficult, of course, to understand what is meant by Union with God, but some idea may be given of what it is intended to mean. If we assume that, whatsoever may have been (apart from the falseness of using a tense, which implies time) the manner of God's creation of the world, the substance of that creation was the conversion by God of His own consciousness into the plural consciousness of separate beings. The great cry of the Indian Deity, 'Oh that I might be many!' gives the idea without the idea of reality.[15]

In this fascinating text Pessoa reveals, almost casually, a telling knowledge of Indian sources. I speculate that he is alluding to the line from the *Chāndogya Upaniṣad* already mentioned—'And it thought to itself: "Let me become many"'[16]—Pessoa presumably having encountered this line in one of the theosophical works he read, such as Annie Besant's *Wisdom of the Upanishads*.[17] Pessoa continues:

> Union with God means therefore the repetition by the Adept of the Divine Act of Creation, by which he is identical with God in act, or manner of act, but, at the same time, an inversion of the Divine Act, by which he is still divided from God, or God's opposite, else he were God Himself and no union were required. The Adept, if he succeeds in making his consciousness one with the consciousness of all things, in making it an unconsciousness (or unselfconsciousness) which is conscious, repeats within himself the Divine Act, which is the conversion of God's individual consciousness into God's plural consciousness in individuals.[18]

---

[14] Other than in this one remark: 'The ego itself, the I in each one of us, is perhaps a divine dimension.' *The Book of Disquiet*, #76.

[15] Centeno, Y. K., ed. *Fernando Pessoa e a Filosofia Hermética - Fragmentos do espólio*. Presença, 1985, p. 77. Arquivo Pessoa, text 637.

[16] *Chāndogya Upaniṣad* 6.2.3. In *The Early Upaniṣads*, p. 247.

[17] Besant, Annie. *Wisdom of the Upanishads*. Madras: Theosophical Publishing House, 1907, pp. 31–2. Besant, noting that the line also appears in the *Taittirīya Upaniṣad*, translates it as 'May I be many' (*Taittirīya* 2.6: 'He had this desire: "Let me multiply myself"'; *The Early Upaniṣads*, p. 305).

[18] Centeno, *Fernando Pessoa e a Filosofia Hermética - Fragmentos do espólio*, p. 77.

Pessoa's marvellous sentence, 'the conversion of God's individual consciousness into God's plural consciousness in individuals', can be paraphrased as stating that a divine self is transformed into a plurality of individual selves, a transformation which renders those individual selves 'identical with God in act' without, of course, entailing the dissolution of God in the process. This is very nearly, though certainly not quite, the same as the idea that individuals are all heteronyms of God (and Pessoa did not, to my knowledge, interconnect his hermeticist speculations with his heteronymic poetry in any significant way). The concept of heteronymy anyway provides us with a way to understand the nature of the 'conversion' in question: just as Pessoa heteronymically 'converts' himself into Caeiro in enactive simulation, so too the cosmic self 'converts' itself, heteronymically, into each and every individual human subject. Pessoa elsewhere writes, 'God is the fact that we exist and that's not all.'[19] Whatever it is that Pessoa himself means by '...and that's not all', the possibility I have been exploring is that we exist and are all heteronyms.

There is a surprisingly strong echo of the same idea in one of the stories by Borges I discussed above, *Everything and Nothing*. Borges writes,

> History adds that before or after he died, he discovered himself standing before God, and said to Him: I, who have been so many men in vain, wish to be one, to be myself. God's voice answered him out of a whirlwind: I, too, am not I. I dreamed the world as you, Shakespeare, dreamed your own work, and among the forms of my dreams are you, who like me are many, yet no one.[20]

What God is given to say here is that he has assumed the heteronym 'Shakespeare', and many other heteronyms besides. Indeed, though this isn't stated explicitly, the presumption is that every individual human subject is a heteronym God has assumed. And in so doing God, self-alienated, has become the ultimate fugitive, 'many, yet no one'.

One might seek to derive a cousin of heteronymic cosmopsychism from heteropsychism. Heteropsychism claims that there are subjects which are heteronyms of other subjects. Perhaps it can even claim that every subject is a heteronym of another subject. Let's suppose, in addition, that every subject is a heteronym of some one other subject. That one is not the cosmos,

---

[19] *The Book of Disquiet*, #22.
[20] Borges, Jorge Luis. *Collected Fictions*, translated by Andrew Hurley. Penguin, 1999, p. 319.

nor is it God; it is an individual who is, heteronymically, every other. We find exactly this conjecture in Andy Weir's short story *The Egg*. God, writing in the first person, addresses the only other character in the second person: ' "There is no one else," I said. "In this universe, there's just you and me." You stared blankly at me. "But all the people on earth…" "All you. Different incarnations of you." "Wait, I'm everyone!?" '[21] Is there not a hint of the same idea in this allusive passage from the seventeenth-century Persian philosopher Mullā Ṣadrā:

> Pythagoras is reported to have said: 'A spiritual essence (*dhātan;* self) shone knowledge upon me, and I asked: Who are you? It said: I am your complete nature.' [What we said] supports this thesis. Oh my beloved, if you were allowed to ascend to levels of your being, you would see a number of beings differing from each other in existence, each of them a completeness of your being which lacks nothing of you, and each one of them referred to as 'I'. This is like in the famous proverb: 'You are I, so who am I?'.[22]

This passage seems to pluralise the ancient notion of the *syzygos,* or divine double, in order to yield an analogue of heteronymic cosmopsychism.

In the popular understanding of Advaita philosophy which took hold in the nineteenth century, the difference between individual selves is an illusion, as, indeed, are those individual selves themselves. Pessoa is aware of this view, which in the secondary literature he read is somewhat astonishingly presented not just as the view of one particular Indian thinker but as the essence of Hindu, and even of Indian, thought as a whole. George Mead is guilty of this elision, writing in his *Quests Old and New,* 'The dominant philosophical thought of India is based, as is well known, on the conviction that there is but one absolute reality and all else is fiction (*māyā*).'[23] In this one sentence, Mead provides an adequate synopsis of the popular understanding of the Advaita metaphysics of Śaṅkara, the one absolute reality being *brahman* and the 'all else' being, most particularly, all individual subjects; but his claim that this is the 'dominant philosophical thought of India' is a vast overgeneralization. Victor Henry, in *Les Littératures de l'Inde,* is

---

[21] Weir, Andy. *The egg.* http://www.galactanet.com/oneoff/theegg_mod.html.

[22] Translation Kaukua, Jari. 'A closed book: the opacity of the human self in Mullā Ṣadrā'. *Vivarium* 52 (2014), pp. 241–60, at p. 251.

[23] Mead, *Quests Old and New,* p. 248. See also Cardiello, Antonio, and Gori, Pietro. 'Nietzsche's and Pessoa's psychological fictionalism'. *Pessoa Plural* 10 (2016), pp. 578–605.

only slightly less sweeping, attributing the view to Vedānta as a whole (a school with many branches, of which Advaita Vedānta is but one and Śaṅkara just one voice within it): 'Pour le Vedānta, l'âme individuelle n'est, encore une fois, qu'une illusion entre toute celles qu'éparpille autour de soi Brahmā le seul vivant' (For the Vedānta, the individual soul is, once again, only one of the illusions that Brahmā [sic], the only living [conscious?] being, scatters around him).[24] Pessoa has underlined this sentence, and, in a remark assigned to the heteronym António Mora, he summarizes what he has taken away from his reading of the secondary literature as being that 'To the Indian the individual soul is one of the many illusions of that divine division we call the world...For the Christian beauty is in everything that clearly makes us feel our personality; to the Oriental in all that transcends our personality.'[25] Another book owned by Pessoa is Jules de Gaultier's De Kant à Nietzsche,[26] in which Gaultier affirms a deep affinity between the philosophies of Hinduism and Kant. Mattia Riccardi suggests that Gaultier's 'fanciful link between Kantianism and Hinduism is based on the idea that both endorse the view that the "real" world is nothing but an "illusion".'[27] However misinformed as to the actual spread of the view, what is more important is that Pessoa does not find it an attractive one, speaking instead of 'the principle, which we already know to be absurd, that the universe is an illusion.'[28]

Ironically, in this rejection of idealism many of Pessoa's contemporaries in India have agreed with him. Thinkers from Hindu schools other than Advaita Vedānta categorically reject the monism and idealism of Śaṅkara, and so do many Advaita philosophers who, writing in pre-independence

[24] Henry, Victor. Les Littératures de l'Inde: sanscrit, pâli, prâcrit. Paris: Hachette, 1904, p. 75.
[25] Lind, Georg Rudolf, and Coelho, Jacinto do Prado, eds. Páginas Íntimas e de Auto-Interpretação. Lisbon: Ática, 1996, p. 243. Arquivo Pessoa, text 3897.
[26] Gaultier, Jules de. De Kant à Nietzsche. Paris: Mercure de France, 1910 (4th edn.); translated by G. M. Spring, From Kant to Nietzsche, New York, 1961. Pessoa's copy is in the Casa Fernando Pessoa.
[27] Riccardi, Mattia. 'António Mora and German philosophy: Between Kant and Nietzsche'. In Pessoa in an Intertextual Web: Influence and Innovation, edited by David Frier. Legenda, 2012, pp. 32–45, at p. 36. The modern Advaita philosopher Krishnachandra Bhattacharya (1875–1949) strongly affirms an affinity between the two systems, as have others, so the link is not quite as 'fanciful' as Riccardi would have us believe. It is an association Pessoa may have assimilated, writing in a note, again attributed to António Mora, 'transcendentalism: hindu system'. Teixeira, Luís Filipe B. ed., Obras de António Mora. Imprensa Nacional-Casa da Moeda, 2002, p. 301.
[28] [o princípio, que já sabemos absurdo, de que o universo é uma ilusão.] Lopes, Teresa Rita, ed. Pessoa por Conhecer-Textos para um Novo Mapa. Lisbon: Estampa, 1990, p. 394. Arquivo Pessoa, text 739.

India, were developing new interpretations of cardinal Advaita claims.[29] Jonathan Schaffer importantly distinguishes between what he calls 'priority' and 'existence' versions of monism, priority monism being the thesis that there is just one basic, foundational object grounding every other, existence monism claiming, more strongly, that this basic object is the one and only concrete object in existence.[30] Modern Advaita philosophers appreciated the point and distanced their interpretations from the popular, idealistic view. Anukulchandra Mukerji, writing in Allahabad in 1938 in his seminal book *The Nature of Self*, says,

> The conclusion we have tried to defend in the foregoing pages may be summarized as follows. All knowledge and experience [appertaining to individual human subjects] has for its ultimate implication an absolutely identical, eternal, infinite, unobjectifiable experience which may be called foundational experience .... If the terms 'self' and 'consciousness' be used, as they are very often used in modern philosophy, in the sense of a relation, then the foundational consciousness cannot be either a self or consciousness. But we have found ample reason to call it consciousness presupposed by all knowledge-events or fragmentary consciousness.[31]

Mukerji is clear that this affirmation of priority cosmopsychism is logically separable from the idealistic and absolutist thesis that nothing other than consciousness exists:

> A word of explanation may be useful at this place in regard to the precise meaning in which consciousness is said to be the *prius* of reality. This doctrine is often interpreted on the idealistic line and supposed to deny the independent existence of the material world apart from consciousness. This, however, would be to raise a highly controversial and difficult problem, and if the priority of consciousness could not be established till the age-long controversy on the relation between the external world and the

---

[29] Even the theosophist Annie Besant interprets *tat tvam asi* as affirming 'the identity in nature of the Universal and the Particular Self', not as that the Universal Self alone exists and the Particular Self is an illusion. *Wisdom of the Upanishads*, p. 4. An Indian thinker to resist the popular view is Aurobindo Ghose, a contemporary of Pessoa and someone who, like Pessoa, was critical of the institutions of the Theosophical Society. Ghose, Aurobindo. *The Life Divine*. Lotus Press, 1942.

[30] Schaffer, Jonathan. 'Monism: the priority of the whole'. *Philosophical Review* 119 (2010), pp. 31–76, at p. 65.

[31] Mukerji, A. C. *The Nature of Self*. The Indian Press, Allahabad 1938, pp. 159, 236.

knowing mind had been settled once and for all in favour of idealism, the Advaita theory of consciousness would naturally stand on a shaky foundation. It is, therefore, important to disassociate the assertion of the priority of consciousness from the idealistic contention and realise clearly that the doctrine of the priority of consciousness is equally compatible with the realistic belief in an independent world.[32]

The thesis that there is one fundamental entity, which Mukerji, in an anticipation of much later work on grounding, describes as 'foundational' and as 'prior', is as compatible with realism as it is with idealism. Mukerji proposes a sophisticated interpretation of Advaita cosmopsychism in which the popular corollary that 'all else is an illusion' is denied.[33]

Heteronymic cosmopsychism agrees with priority monism in rejecting a monistic existence thesis, differing from it as to the nature of the grounding relation, and sidestepping the problems that bedevil priority cosmopsychism because its grounding relation is not one of mereological decomposition. A different response to those problems, and one which has gained some traction in contemporary debates, has been to claim that the cosmos is not itself a personal self because it does not have a perspective, but that it somehow nevertheless provides an impersonal conscious ground for individual personal subjects. Let me call this view 'impersonal cosmopsychism'. Contemporary advocates of this view also claim to find support in Advaita Vedānta, interpreting *brahman* now as impersonal consciousness. There is already a suggestion of the idea in Mukerji's hesitation as to whether the 'foundational consciousness' can itself be a self, if selves are essentially 'relational'. Advocates of impersonal cosmopsychism typically assume that the foundational consciousness cannot be a self because it doesn't have a spatio-temporal perspective. Yet, as we have seen, it is perfectly possible for there to be aperspectival selves: a self, for Pessoa, is the occupant of a phenomenal subject position and the index of a manner of phenomenal resonance.

---

[32] Mukerji, *The Nature of Self*, pp. 113–14. Still another critic is Surendranath Dasgupta (1887–1952), who explicitly uses the term 'ground', saying that what Śaṅkara affirms is 'that the entity denoted by the term Brahman in the Upaniṣads was the ultimate reality which is the underlying ground of all our experience and all phenomena as such.' Dasgupta, Surendranath. 'Māyā of Śaṅkara and his followers'. In his *Philosophical Essays*. Calcutta, 1941, pp. 337–8.

[33] Luca Gaspari argues that Advaita Vedānta is not a type of cosmopsychism because it is committed to the existence thesis. This point is well taken as applied to popular representations of Śaṅkara's reading of Advaita, including those Pessoa was exposed to, and is itself the reason modern Advaitins provide more nuanced interpretations. Gaspari, Luca. 'Priority cosmopsychism and the Advaita Vedānta'. *Philosophy East and West* 69 (2019), pp. 130–42.

Impersonal cosompsychists take the foundational consciousness of the cosmos instead to consist in reflexive self-awareness, or, drawing on a metaphor of illumination, in self-illuminating luminous awareness.[34] Yet, as we have also seen, reflexive self-awareness, being attenuated, cannot serve as a ground for selves. Impersonal cosmopsychism faces exactly the same challenge as confronts those psychological constructivists who think one can build subjects out of impersonal psychological elements, namely that it is a mystery how to ground individual selves in any sort of psychological stuff which does not itself already exhibit subjectivity.

Pessoa himself considers, and rejects, impersonal cosmopsychism. In a note on the flyleaf at the end of his copy of George Mead's *Quests Old and New*, which I have quoted before, he writes that

> there is no such thing as consciousness; that is, there is no such thing as consciousness itself. There are only the conscious. Only when consciousness obeys the law of plurality which is the 1st Law of Reality, then C[onscious]ness ceases to exist as consciousness, it comes to exist as Reality, it comes into being, *tout court*. There is no meaning of Consciousness, but only of the conscious I, only of the sensual error, only of the I itself.[35]

Pessoa here denies that there is any such thing as impersonal consciousness, or, as I put it before, as a selfless mind.

Heteronymic cosmopsychism is, like heteropsychism, a 'modest' solution to the problem of grounding subjects, and the great virtue of modesty in the philosophy of mind is that such mysteries are firmly and definitively held at bay. Only subjects can create subjects, and the mechanism by which they do so is one of heteronymic simulation. So the phrase for which, in this book, we have striven so hard to find an elucidation, the phrase 'another I,' does indeed perfectly encapsulate the essence of Pessoa's philosophy of self.

---

[34] Albahari, Miri. 'Perennial idealism: A mystical solution to the mind-body problem'. *Philosophers' Imprint* 19 (2019), pp. 1–37. Albahari draws heavily on modern Advaita Vedānta in support of her claims, especially the ideas of Nisargadatta Maharaja and Ramana Maharshi.

[35] Transcription and translation: Cardiello, Antonio, and Gori, Pietro. 'Nietzsche's and Pessoa's psychological fictionalism'. *Pessoa Plural* 10 (2016), pp. 578–605, at p. 594.

Postscript

Among the many fragmentary texts that remain as Pessoa's literary bequest are notes for what may have been intended as a philosophical novel. Dating from 1914, the following sketch is of particular interest:

> I do not know who I am, what soul I have. When I speak with sincerity, I do not know with what sincerity I speak. I am variously other than a self that I do not know exists (if it is those others)...I feel multifaceted. I am like a room with innumerable fantastic mirrors that distort false reflections, a single previous reality that is not in any and is in all. As the pantheist feels as if a wave, star, and flower, I feel as if various beings. I feel myself living other lives, in myself, incompletely, as if my being participated in all men, incompletely in each, individuated by a sum of nonselves synthesized into a dummy self.[1]

All the major themes in his more developed writing are foretold in this short sketch. There is already an anticipation of the separation between forumnal and heteronymic self-awareness, of a distinction between the self that possesses mental states and a sense of agency, and an impersonal fugitive that stands watching. There are strong intimations of self-alienation, of moods that are me and yet are not me. The beginnings of subject multiplicity are already here too, a fractured self and even an allusion to what would become the infinity room of Yayoi Kusama, here used to multiply the self rather than eliminate it.[2] And, finally, there is the barest hint of the view I have termed heteronymic cosmopsychism, a single self whose many heteronyms are us.

---

[1] Zenith, Richard, ed, with the collaboration of Manuela Parreira da Silva. *Escritos Autobiográficos, Automáticos, e de Reflexão Pessoal*. Lisbon, 2003, p. 151. I thank Austin Simoes-Gomes for assisting me with this text.

[2] Pessoa could, perhaps, have been thinking of the Mirror Hall built by the third patriarch of the Huayan tradition, Fazang (643–712), in which ten mirrors surrounding a Buddha statue produced an infinite number of Buddha reflections.

Virtual Subjects, Fugitive Selves: Fernando Pessoa and his Philosophy. Jonardon Ganeri,
Oxford University Press (2021). © Jonardon Ganeri.
DOI: 10.1093/oso/9780198864684.001.0001

Pessoa would go on to train himself to become an expert in the arts of the imagination. His first-personal 'meditations' went much further than those of Descartes, and he took himself to the very limits of imaginative possibility. His phenomenology, so much more poetic than that of the prosaic Husserl, allows us to feel afresh just what an extraordinary thing it is to be a subjective being in the world. For 'in this metallic age...only a relentless cultivation of our ability to dream, to analyse and to captivate can prevent our personality from degenerating into nothing'.[3] He developed a new *askesis*, a set of techniques, a technology of the self, with the aim of bringing the fugitivity of self-consciousness to the fore, calling the entire method depersonalization and demonstrating with great clarity how to distinguish it from several, closely similar, ideas that could also go by the same name, such as that of centrelessness in the landscape of presence and that of an emptiness at the centre. And, most famously, he discovered that there is a way to simulate other I's within oneself, to virtualize and multiply the subject position.

In his multifaceted writings about these discoveries, from heteronymic poetry to the prose antinovel *The Book of Disquiet*, and from letters, prefaces, and philosophical sketches to neopagan and hermeticist reflections, Pessoa provides us with a new vocabulary for the self, a new repertoire of conceptual tools for interpreting and analysing subjectivity: heteronymy, the fugitive, landscapes, dreaming, intersection, orthonyms, and much else besides. He thought of himself as forging a new science for studying the subjective mind: 'What really astounds me is that [ordinary scientists] don't realize there are things hidden in the cracks of knowledge—things of the soul and consciousness—that can also be classified'.[4]

Pessoa believed himself to be exploring the outer reaches of experiential possibility. And yet he did not consider the possibility of nested and circular heteronymy, nor that of uncentred minds, nor the implications of total sensory deprivation. Nor did he fully explore the idea that we might all be heteronyms of some single cosmic self. And yet his theory is quite rich enough to allow for analysis of these topics and thus to provide new insights into some of the trickiest puzzles about the self in the global history of philosophy. In applying Pessoa's philosophy of the subject to puzzles in the writings of Buddhist, Daoist, Persian, and Hindu philosophers, and to matters of interpretation in conceptual art, musicology, and literary theory, it has turned out that we can gain a more profound understanding of the nature of the self than has been possible before.

---

[3] *The Book of Disquiet*, #369.   [4] *The Book of Disquiet*, #378.

Bibliography

A. Pessoa

(A_1) Online Archives

Arquivo Pessoa, http://arquivopessoa.net. An archive of Pessoa's texts, fragments, and poetry.

Casa Fernando Pessoa, http://bibliotecaparticular.casafernandopessoa.pt/index/aut/index.htm. Scans of the books in Pessoa's personal library with his marginal notes.

LdoD Archive, https://ldod.uc.pt. The sketches constituting *The Book of Disquiet*, cross-referenced against major editions.

(A_2) Print Materials

Centeno, Y. K., ed. *Fernando Pessoa e a Filosofia Hermética—Fragmentos do espólio*. Presença, 1985.

Pessoa, Fernando. *Fernando Pessoa & Co.: Selected Poems*, edited and translated by Richard Zenith. Grove Press, 1999.

Pessoa, Fernando. *The Book of Disquiet*, edited and translated by Richard Zenith. Penguin, 2002.

Pessoa, Fernando. *A Little Larger than the Entire Universe: Selected Poems*, edited and translated by Richard Zenith. Penguin, 2006.

Pessoa, Fernando. *The Selected Prose of Fernando Pessoa*, edited and translated by Richard Zenith. Grove Press, 2007.

Pessoa, Fernando. *Philosophical Essays: A Critical Edition*, edited and translated by Nuno Ribeiro. Contra Mundum Press, 2012.

Pessoa, Fernando. *The Book of Disquiet*, edited by Jerónimo Pizarro and translated by Margaret Jull Costa. New Directions, 2013.

Pessoa, Fernando. *The Transformation Book*, edited and translated by Nuno Ribeiro. Contra Mundum Press, 2014.

Pizarro, Jerónimo, ed. *Sensacionismo e Outros Ismos*. Vol. X of the critical edition. Imprensa Nacional-Casa da Moeda, 2009.

Quadros, António, and Dalila Pereira da Costa, eds. *Obra Poética e em Prosa*, Lello & Irmão Editores, 1986, vol. 2.

Sabino, Maria do Rosário Marques, and Sereno, Adelaide Maria Monteiro, eds., *Novas Poesias Inéditas. Obras completas de Fernando Pessoa*, no. 10. Lisbon: Ática, 1973.

Teixeira, Luís Filipe B. ed., *Obras de António Mora*. Imprensa Nacional-Casa da Moeda, 2002.

Zenith, Richard, ed. *Escritos Autobiográficos, Automáticos, e de Reflexão Pessoal*. Edited with the collaboration of Manuela Parreira da Silva. Lisbon: Assírio & Alvim, 2003.

B. On Pessoa

BBC World Service. 'Fernando Pessoa: the man who multiplied himself'. 9 September 2019; https://www.bbc.co.uk/programmes/w3csyp56.

Billiani, Francesca. 'Tabucchi in search of Pessoa's heteronymous body'. In *Embodying Pessoa: Corporeality, Gender, Sexuality*, edited by Anna Klobucka and Mark Sabine. University of Toronto Press, 2007, pp. 273–92.

Borges, Paulo. 'As coisas são coisas?' *Pessoa Plural* 9 (2006), pp. 107–27.

Braga, Druarte Drumond. 'Um roteiro pessoano sobre a Índia'. *Pessoa Plural* 10 (2016), pp. 11–36.

Cardiello, Antonio. 'Abysmo y nada absoluto: confluencias budistas en el pensamiento de Fernando Pessoa e Nishida Kataro'. In *El Pensar Poético de Fernando Pessoa*, edited by Pablo López and Fernando Quindós. Madrid: Manuscritos, 2010, pp. 83–170.

Cardiello, Antonio. 'Os Orientes de Fernando Pessoa: adenda'. *Pessoa Plural* 10 (2016), pp. 128–85.

Cardiello, Antonio, and Gori, Pietro. 'Nietzsche's and Pessoa's psychological fictionalism'. *Pessoa Plural* 10 (2016), pp. 578–605.

Castro, Mariana Gray de. 'Pessoa, Coleridge, homens de Porlock e dias triunfais'. *Revista Estranhar Pessoa* 1 (2014), pp. 58–70.

Costineau, Thomas. *An Unwritten Novel: Fernando Pessoa's The Book of Disquiet*. Dalkey Archive Press, 2013.

Courteau, Joanna. 'The quest for identity in Pessoa's orthonymous poetry'. *In The Man who Never Was: Essays on Fernando Pessoa*, edited by George Moneiro. Gavea-Brown Pubns, 1982, pp. 93–108.

Dix, Steffen. 'The plurality of gods and man, or "The aesthetic attitude in all its pagan splendor" in Fernando Pessoa'. *The Pluralist* 5 (2010), pp. 73–93.

Ferrari, Patricio. 'Pessoa and Borges: In the margins of Milton'. *Variaciones Borges* 40 (2015), pp. 3–21.

Frow, John. *Character and Person*. Oxford, 2014.

Ganeri, Jonardon. 'Illusions of immortality'. In *Imaginations of Death and Beyond in India and Europe*, edited by Sudhir Kakar and Günter Blamberger. Delhi, 2018, pp. 35–45.

Ganeri, Jonardon. 'Pessoa's imaginary India'. In *Fernando Pessoa & Philosophy*, edited by Bartholomew Ryan, Giovanbattista Tusa, and Antonio Cardiello. Roman & Littlefield, 2021.

Jackson, David. *Adverse Genres in Fernando Pessoa*. Oxford, 2010.

Kotowicz, Zbigniew. *Fernando Pessoa: Voices of a Nomadic Soul*. Shearsman Press, 2008.

Mahr, Greg. 'Pessoa, life narrative, and the dissociative process'. *Biography* 21 (1998), pp. 24–9.

Marder, Michael. 'Phenomenology of distraction, or, Attention in the fissuring of time and space'. *Research in Phenomenology* 41 (2011), pp. 396–419.

Maunsell, Jerome Boyd. 'The hauntings of Fernando Pessoa'. *Modernism/Modernity* 19 (2012), pp. 115–37.

Medeiros, Paulo de. *Pessoa's Geometry of the Abyss: Modernity and The Book of Disquiet*. Routledge, 2017.

Miranda, Rui Gonçalves. *Personal Infinitive: Inflecting Fernando Pessoa*. Critical, Cultural & Communications Press, 2017.

Mota, Pedro da. 'A Caminho do Oriente: apontamentos de Pessoa sobre Teosofia e espiritualidades da Índia'. *Pessoa Plural* 10 (2016), pp. 230–51.

Pizarro, Jerónimo. 'Fernando Pessoa: Not one but many isms'. In *Portuguese Modernisms: Multiple Perspectives on Literature and the Visual Arts*, edited by Steffen Dix and Jerónimo Pizarro. Legenda, 2011, pp. 24–41.

Pizarro, Jerónimo, Ferrari, Patricio, and Cardiello, Antonio. 'Os orientes de Fernando Pessoa'. *Cultura Entre Culturas* 3 (2011), pp. 148–85.

Riccardi, Mattia. 'António Mora and German philosophy: between Kant and Nietzsche'. In *Pessoa in an Intertextual Web: Influence and Innovation*, edited by David Frier. Legenda, 2012, pp. 32–45.

Sabine, Mark. 'Saramago's "other" Pessoas and "Pessoan" others: Heteronymic creation and the ethics of alterity'. In *Pessoa in an Intertextual Web: Influence and Innovation*, edited by David Frier. Legenda, 2012, pp. 148–71.

Sadlier, Darlene. *An Introduction to Fernando Pessoa: Modernism and the Paradoxes of Authorship*. University Press of Florida, 2009.

Slaby, Jan. 'Living in the moment. Boredom and the meaning of existence in Heidegger and Pessoa'. *Yearbook for Eastern and Western Philosophy* (2) 2017, pp. 235–56.

Stevens, Dana. 'To pretend is to know oneself'. In *Embodying Pessoa: Corporeality, Gender, Sexuality*, edited by Anna Klobucka and Mark Sabine. University of Toronto Press, 2007, pp. 39–51.

Visser, Rehan. 'Fernando Pessoa's art of living: ironic multiplicities, multiple ironies'. *Philosophical Forum* 50 (2019), pp. 435–545.

Zenith, Richard. 'Alberto Caeiro as Zen heteronym'. *Portuguese Literary and Cultural Studies* 3 (1999), pp. 101–9.

C. Philosophy

Adamson, Peter, and Benevich, Fedor. 'The thought experimental method: Avicenna's flying man argument'. *Journal of the American Philosophical Association* 4 (2018), pp. 147–64.

Agamben, Giorgio. *Remnants of Auschwitz: The Witness and the Archive*. Zone Books, 1999.

Albahari, Miri. 'Beyond cosmopsychism and the great I am: how the world might be grounded in universal "Advaitic" consciousness'. In *The Routledge Handbook of Panpsychism*, edited by William Seager. Routledge, 2020, pp. 119–130.

Albahari, Miri. 'Perennial idealism: A mystical solution to the mind-body problem'. *Philosophers' Imprint* 19 (2019), pp. 1–37.

Amiel, Henri-Frédéric. *Fragments d'un journal intime*. Paris, 1885. Translated as *Amiel's Journal* by Mary A. Ward. New York, 1889, two volumes.

Anscombe, G. E. M. 'The first person'. In *Mind and Language*, edited by Samuel Guttenplan. Oxford, 1975, pp. 45–65.

Aung, Shwe Zan, trans. *Compendium of Philosophy*. London: Pali Text Society, 1910.

Bayne, Timothy, and Hohwy, Jakob. 'Modes of consciousness'. In *Finding Consciousness: The Neuroscience, Ethics, and Law of Severe Brain Damage*, edited by Walter Sinnott-Armstrong. Oxford, 2016.

Bayne, Timothy, and Montague, Michael, eds. *Cognitive Phenomenology*. Oxford, 2011.

Besant, Annie. *Wisdom of the Upanishads*. Theosophical Publishing House, 1907.

Black, Deborah. 'Avicenna on self-awareness and knowing that one knows'. In *The Unity of Science in the Arabic Tradition*, edited by S. Rahman et al. Springer, 2008, pp. 63–87.

Braude, Stephen. *First Person Plural*. Routledge, 1991.

Brüntrup, Godehard, and Jaskola, Ludwig, eds., *Panpsychism: Contemporary Perspectives*. Oxford, 2016.

Chakrabarti, Arindam. 'Arguing from synthesis to self: Utpaladeva and Abhinavagupta respond to Buddhist no-self'. In *Hindu and Buddhist Ideas in Dialogue: Self and No-Self*, edited by Irina Kuznetsova, Jonardon Ganeri, and Chakravarthi Ram-Prasad. Routledge, 2012, pp. 199–216.

Chalmers, David. 'Panpsychism and panprotopsychism'. In *Panpsychism: Contemporary Perspectives*, edited by Godehard Brüntrup and Ludwig Jaskola. Oxford, 2016, pp. 19–48.

Cheng, Kai-Yuan. 'Self and the dream of the butterfly in the *Zhuangzi*. *Philosophy East and West* 64 (2014), pp. 563–97.

Coleman, Sam. 'The real combination problem: panpsychism, micro-subjects, and emergence'. *Erkenntnis* 79 (2014), pp. 19–44.

Coleman, Sam. 'Panpsychism and neutral monism: how to make up one's mind'. *Panpsychism: Contemporary Perspectives*, edited by Godehard Brüntrup and Ludwig Jaskola. Oxford, 2016, pp. 249–82.

Correia, Fabrice, and Schnieder, Benjamin, eds. *Metaphysical Grounding: Understanding the Structure of Reality*. Cambridge, 2012.

Crites, Stephen. 'Pseudonymous authorship as art and act'. In *Kierkegaard: A Collection of Critical Essays*, edited by Josiah Thompson. Anchor Books, 1972, pp. 183–229.

Dasgupta, Surendranath. 'Māyā of Śaṅkara and his followers'. In his *Philosophical Essays*. Calcutta, 1941, pp. 332–49.

Dennett, Daniel. 'Where am I?' In his *Brainstorms*. MIT Press, 1981, pp. 310–23.

Dreyfus, Hubert. 'Review of *The Embodied Mind*'. *Mind* 102 (1993), pp. 542–6.

DSM-5. *The Diagnostic and Statistical Manual of Mental Disorders*. American Psychiatric Association, 2013.

Dummett, Michael. *The Seas of Language*. Oxford, 1993.

Ferran, Íngrid Vendrell. 'Narrative fiction as philosophical exploration: A case study of self-envy and akrasia'. In *Literature as Thought Experiment? Perspectives from Philosophy and Literary Studies*, edited by Falk Bornmüller, Johannes Franzen, and Mathis Lessau. Brill, 2019, pp. 123–37.

Frege, Gottlob. *The Foundations of Arithmetic*, translated by J. L. Austin. Northwestern University Press, 1980.

Frege, Gottlob. 'On Sense and reference'. In *Translations from the Philosophical Writings of Gottlob Frege*, edited by Peter Geach and Max Black. Blackwell, 1960, pp. 56–78.

Ganeri, Jonardon. 'Self-intimation, memory and personal identity'. *Journal of Indian Philosophy* 27 (1999), pp. 469–83.

Ganeri, Jonardon. *The Concealed Art of the Soul*. Oxford, 2007.

Ganeri, Jonardon. *The Self: Naturalism, Consciousness, and the First-Person Stance*. Oxford, 2012.

Ganeri, Jonardon. *Attention, Not Self*. Oxford, 2017.

Gaspari, Luca. 'Priority cosmopsychism and the Advaita Vedānta'. *Philosophy East and West* 69 (2019), pp. 130–42.

Gaultier, Jules de. *De Kant à Nietzsche*. Paris: Mercure de France, 1920 (4th edn.). Translation: *From Kant to Nietzsche*, translated by G. M. Spring. New York: The Wisdom Library, 1961.

Gendler, Tamar. *Intuition, Imagination, & Philosophical Methodology*. Oxford, 2010.

Ghose, Aurobindo. *The Life Divine*. Lotus Press, 1942.

Goff, Philip. *Consciousness and Fundamental Reality*. Oxford, 2017.

Goldman, Alvin. *Simulating Minds: The Philosophy, Psychology and Neuroscience of Mindreading*. Oxford, 2006.

Graham, George. *The Disordered Mind*. Routledge, 2010.

Guillot, Marie. 'I me mine: on a confusion concerning the subjective character of experience'. *Review of Philosophy and Psychology* 8 (2017), pp. 23–53.

Hattori, Masaaki. *Dignāga on Perception*. Harvard, 1966.

Henry, Victor. *Les Littératures de l'Inde: sanscrit, pâli, prâcrit*. Paris, Hachette, 1904.

Hill, Christopher. *Sensations: A Defence of Type Materialism*. Cambridge, 1991.

Hill, Christopher. *Consciousness*. Cambridge, 2009.

Hung, Jenny. 'The theory of the self in the *Zhuangzi*: A Strawsonian interpretation'. *Philosophy East and West* 69.2 (2019), pp. 376–94.

Hurlburt, Russell, and Akhter, Sarah. 'The descriptive experience sampling method'. *Phenomenology and the Cognitive Sciences* 5 (2006), pp. 271–301.

Jackson, Frank. 'What Mary didn't know'. *The Journal of Philosophy* 83 (1986), pp. 291–5.

James, William. *A Pluralistic Universe: Hibbert Lectures*. Floating Press, 1909.

Johnston, Mark. *Surviving Death*. Princeton, 2010.

Kaukua, Jari. 'A closed book: the opacity of the human self in Mullā Ṣadrā'. *Vivarium* 52 (2014), pp. 241–60.

Kaukua, Jari. *Self-Awareness in Islamic Philosophy: Avicenna and Beyond*. Cambridge, 2015.

Kierkegaard, Søren. 'A first and last declaration'. In his *Concluding Unscientific Postscript*, translated by Alastair Hannay. Cambridge, 2009, pp. 527–31.

Kim, Jaegwon. 'Lonely souls: causality and substance dualism'. In *Soul, Body, and Survival: Essays in the Metaphysics of Human Persons*, edited by Kevin Corocan. Cornell, 2001, pp. 30–43.

Kriegel, Uriah. *Subjective Consciousness: A Self-Representational Theory*. Oxford, 2009.

Levine, Joseph. *Purple Haze: The Puzzle of Consciousness*. Oxford, 2001.

Levine, Joseph. 'Two kinds of access'. *Behavioral and Brain Sciences* 30 (2007), pp. 514–15.

Lewis David. 'What experience teaches'. *Proceedings of the Russellian Society* 13 (1988), pp. 29–50.

Lusthaus, Dan. 'A pre-Dharmakīrti discussion of Dignāga preserved in Chinese translation: the *Buddhabhumy-upadeśa*'. *Journal of Buddhist Studies* 6 (2009), pp. 19–81.

Lycan, William. 'The superiority of HOP to HOT'. In *Higher-Order Theories of Consciousness*, edited by Rocco J. Gennaro. John Benjamins Publishing Co., 2004, pp. 93–114.

Mach, Ernst. 'The analysis of the sensations: antimetaphysical'. *The Monist* 1 (1890), pp. 48–68.

Mead, G. R. S. *Quests Old and New*. G. Bell & Sons, 1913.

Metzinger, Thomas. *The Ego Tunnel: The Science of the Mind and the Myth of the Self*. Basic Books, 2009.

Montero, Barbara. *Thought in Action: Expertise and the Conscious Mind*. Oxford, 2016.

Mukerji, A. C. *The Nature of Self*. The Indian Press, Allahabad, 1938.

Nagasawa, Yujin, and Wager, Khai. 'Panpsychism and priority cosmopsychism'. In *Panpsychism: Contemporary Perspectives*, edited by Godehard Brüntrup and Ludwig Jaskola. Oxford, 2016, pp. 113–29.

Nagel, Thomas. 'What is it like to be a bat?' *The Philosophical Review* 83.4 (1974), pp. 435–50.

Ñāṇamoli, Bhikkhu, trans. *The Path of Purification: Visuddhimagga by Bhadantācariya Buddhaghosa*. Kandy: Buddhist Publication Society, 1991.

Nietzsche, Friedrich. *The Birth of Tragedy*, translated by Douglas Smith. Oxford, 2008.

Noyes, Arthur P., and Kolb, Lawrence Coleman. *Modern Clinical Psychiatry*. Philadelphia: W. B. Saunders, 6th edn.,1964.

O'Shaughnessy, Brian. *Consciousness and the World*. Oxford, 2002.

Parfit, Derek. *Reasons and Persons*. Oxford, 1984.

Paul, Laurie. *Transformative Experience*. Oxford, 2014.

Pitt, David. 'The phenomenology of cognition, or, what is it like to think that *p*?' *Philosophy and Phenomenological Research* 69 (2004), pp. 1–36.

Prosser, Simon, and Recanati, François, eds., *Immunity to Error through Misidentification: New Essays*. Cambridge, 2012.

Radden, Jennifer. 'Multiple selves'. In *The Oxford Handbook of the Self*, edited by Shaun Gallagher. Oxford, 2011, pp. 548–71.

Roelofs, Luke. *Combining Minds: How to Think about Composite Subjectivity*. Oxford, 2019.

Sacks, Oliver. *The Man who Mistook his Wife for a Hat and Other Clinical Tales*. Harper Perennial, New York, 1990.

Schaffer, Jonathan. 'Monism: the priority of the whole'. *Philosophical Review* 119 (2010), pp. 31–76.

Shani, Itay. 'Cosmopsychism: A holistic approach to the metaphysics of consciousness'. *Philosophical Papers* 44 (2015), pp. 389–437.

Shani, Itay, and Keppler, Joachim. 'Beyond combination: How cosmic consciousness grounds ordinary experience'. *Journal of the American Philosophical Association* 4/3 (2018), pp. 390–410.

Siewert, Charles. *The Significance of Consciousness*. Princeton University Press, 1998.

Simeon, Daphne, and Abuge, Jeffrey. *Feeling Unreal: Depersonalization Disorder and the Loss of Self*. Oxford, 2006.

Stang, Charles. *Our Divine Double*. Harvard, 2016.

Stoljar, Daniel. 'The semantics of "what it's like" and the nature of consciousness'. *Mind* 125 (2016), pp. 1161–98.

Thompson, Evan. Waking, *Dreaming, Being: Self and Consciousness in Neuroscience, Meditation and Philosophy*. Columbia, 2014.

Tillemans, Tom. 'What would it be like to be selfless? Hināyānist versions, Māhāyānist versions, and Derek Parfit'. *Asiatische Studien* 50 (1996), pp. 835–52.

Valberg, Jerome J. *Dream, Death, and the Self*. Princeton, 2007.

Varela, Francisco, Thompson, Evan, and Rosch, Eleanor. *The Embodied Mind: Cognitive Science and Human Experience*. MIT Press, 1991. Revised edition, 2016.

Watzl, Sebastian. *Structuring Mind: The Nature of Attention and How it Shapes Consciousness*. Oxford, 2017.

Weil, Simone. *First and Last Notebooks*, translated by Richard Rees. London: Oxford University Press, 1970.

Weil, Simone. *Gravity and Grace*, translated by Emma Crawford and Mario von der Ruhr. Routledge, 2002.

Weil, Simone. *Waiting for God*, translated by Emma Craufurd. HarperCollins, 2009.

Williams, Bernard. 'Imagination and the self'. In his *Problems of the Self*. Cambridge, 1973, 26–45.

Wittgenstein, Ludwig. *Tractatus Logico-Philosophicus*, translated by C. K. Ogden. Routledge, 1922.

Wu, Wayne. 'Introspection as attention and action'. Forthcoming.

Zahavi, Dan. *Self and Other: Exploring Subjectivity, Empathy, and Shame*. Oxford, 2015.

Zahavi, Dan. 'Consciousness and selfhood: Getting clearer on for-me-ness and mineness'. In *The Oxford Handbook of the Philosophy of Consciousness*, edited by Uriah Kriegel. Oxford, 2020, chapter 29.

Zahavi, Dan. 'Reflexivity, transparency and illusionism'. *Protosociology* 36 (2020), pp. 142–56.

Zahavi, Dan, and Kriegel, Uriah. 'For-me-ness: What it is and what it is not'. In *Philosophy of Mind and Phenomenology: Conceptual and Empirical Approaches*, edited by Daniel O. Dahlstrom, Andreas Elpidorou, and Walter Hopp. Routledge, 2015, pp. 36–55.

Zeimbekis, John, and Raftopoulos, Athanassios, eds. *The Cognitive Penetrability of Perception: New Philosophical Perspectives*. Oxford, 2015.

D. Literature

Akutagawa Ryūnosuke. *Rashōmon and Other Stories*, translated by Kojima Takashi. Tuttle Publishing, 2011.

Borges, Jorge Luis. *Collected Fictions*, translated by Andrew Hurley. Penguin, 1999.

Cortázar, Julio. '*La noche boca arriba (The night face up)*'. In *The End of the Game, and Other Stories*, translated by Paul Blackburn. Pantheon,1963.

Cortázar, Julio. *Hopscotch: A Novel*, translated by Gregory Rabassa. Pantheon, 1987.

Eshun, Kodwo. *More Brilliant than the Sun: Adventures in Sonic Fiction*. Quartet Books, 1999.

Faulkner, William. *As I Lay Dying*. Random House, 1990.

Kusama, Yayoi. *Infinity Net: The Autobiography of Yayoi Kusama*. Tate Publishing, 2011.

Lem, Stanisław. *Dialogi*. Kraków, 1957.

Manganelli, Giorgio. *La Notte*. Milan: Adelphi, 1996.

Mauni. *Mauni: A Writer's Writer, Short Stories*, translated by Lakshmi Holmstrom. Katha, 1997.

Morimura Yasumasa. Original screenplay for *My Art, My Story, My Art History—A Sympósion on Self-Portraits. Egó Sympósion*. Japan Society, New York, 2018, pp. 148–59.

Olivelle, Patrick, trans. *The Early Upaniṣads*. Oxford, 1998.

Pamuk, Orhan. *My Name is Red*, translated by Erdağ M. Göknar. Faber & Faber, 2001.

Patton, Laurie, trans. *The Bhagavad Gītā*. Penguin Classics, 2008.

Proust, Marcel. *Remembrance of Things Past*, translated by C. K. Scott Moncrieff and Terence Kilmartin. Random House, 1982.

Reddell, Trace. 'Ethnoforgery and Outsider Afrofuturism'. *Dancecult: Journal of Electronic Dance Music Culture* 5 (2013), pp. 88–112.

Saramago, José. *The Year of the Death of Ricardo Reis*, translated by Giovanni Ponteiro. Harvill Press, 1988.

Saramago, José. *The Notebook*, translated by Amanda Hopkinson and Daniel Hahn. London, Verso, 2010.

Smith, John, trans. *The Mahābhārata*. Penguin Classics, 2009.

Tabucchi, Antonio. *Pereira Declares*, translated by Patrick Creagh. New Direction, 1997.

Tagore, Rabindranath. *Gītāñjali and Fruit-gathering*, with an introduction by W. B. Yeats. Leipzig, 1922.

Tagore, Rabindranath. *Poems*. London, 1925.

Unamuno, Miguel de. *Mist*, translated by Warner Fite. University of Illinois Press, 1955.

Unamuno, Miguel de. 'The Novel of Don Sandalio, Chess player'. In *Fictions*, vol. 7 of the *Selected Works of Miguel de Unamuno*, translated by Anthony Kerrigan. Princeton, 1976, pp. 183–226.

Weir, Andy. *The egg*. http://www.galactanet.com/oneoff/theegg_mod.html.

Ziporyn, Brook, trans. *Zhuangzi: The Essential Writings*. Hackett, 2009.

Index

For the benefit of digital users, indexed terms that span two pages (e.g., 52–53) may, on occasion, appear on only one of those pages.

names
  direct reference theory of 101, 102n.11
  machine 31
  see also heteronym, homopseudonym,
    orthonym, polyonym, pseudonym
nesting, heteronymic 123–9
Nietzsche, Friedrich 27, 27n.14
  The Birth of Tragedy 50–1
Nyāya 'syllogism,' 107–8

O'Shaughnessy, Brian
  on the 'mythical S' 91–2
orthonym 6–7, 16, 19, 93–8, 100–2,
    128–9, 150; see also
    homopseudonym

Pamuk, Orhan 11, 24, 76–7
panpsychism
  Buddhist 132–5
  definition of 130–1
  Pessoa on 131–2, 135–6
  subject combination problem
    for 25n.9, 131–2
Paul, Laurie 52–3
personal identity 24, 33
persons
  as higher-order individuals 33–4,
    109, 132–3
  protean 24, 32
perspectival centres 79–80, 110
  as partial views 140–1
  field vs. observer 89n.6
  first-person 121, 130–2, 136
  multiply occupied 38–9
  not combinable 25, 140–1
  vs. positional centres 141, 147–8
Pessoa, Fernando
  Book of Disquiet, The, Bernardo Soares as
    semi-heteronymic protagonist of
    6–7, 7n.19, 19, 41–2, 73–4,
    94–5, 141–2
  intellectual biography of vii, 3n.1,
    12n.11, 149–50
  Mariner, The 124–5
  neopaganism, his interest in vii, 139n.5,
    141–2, 150
  non-European philosophy, his interest
    in 107–8, 118n.3, 142
  Philosophical Essays 131–2
  poems (index locorum)
    'Autopsychography' 72–3

'Countless lives inhabit us' 7–8, 23,
    26–7, 62–3
'I don't know who my soul is' 8
'I have built my temple—wall and
    face,' 80–1
Slanting Rain 36–8
'Time's passage' 54
pre-heteronymic vii, 41–2, 102
Transformation Book, The 7n.19
triumphal day, his 46
phenomenality, dimensions of 59, 92;
    see also manifestation
phenomenology
  cognitive 122
  fugitive 73–5
  sensory, see sensation; phenomenality
Phenomenology, schools of
  analytical (Pessoa) 22, 42–3,
    49–53, 83
  empirical 41
  experiential (Heidegger) 41n.2
  transcendental (Husserl) 41
Pintor, Santa-Rita 38n.11
Pitt, David 122n.16
Pizarro, Jerónimo 36n.6, 54n.26, 107n.1
Plato 99–100
polyonym 10
Porlock Man, the 76–7
positional conception of self, the 116,
    132, 135
  as distinct from horizonal conception of
    self 78, 81
  availability in aperspectival
    consciousness 141
  availability in sensory deprivation
    118–20, 122
  content of 88–90
  defined 68–9
  in Pessoa 69–70
  marked in Classical Chinese 126–7
  role in solution to the enigma of
    heteronymy 71, 87, 139–40
  role in analysis of the fugitive self 71, 73,
    77, 92, 111
  Simone Weil's opposition to 108, 113
priority monism 134, 145–8
Proust, Marcel 26–7, 32
pseudonym
  as distinct from heteronym 4, 14, 31
  homopseudonym 97n.14
  Kierkegaard's 10